THIS BOOK BELONGS TO:

MINECRAFT SECRETS & CHEATS ANNUAL 2019
ISBN: 978-1-78106-679-9

MINECRAFT
SECRETS & CHEATS
ANNUAL
2019

CONTENTS

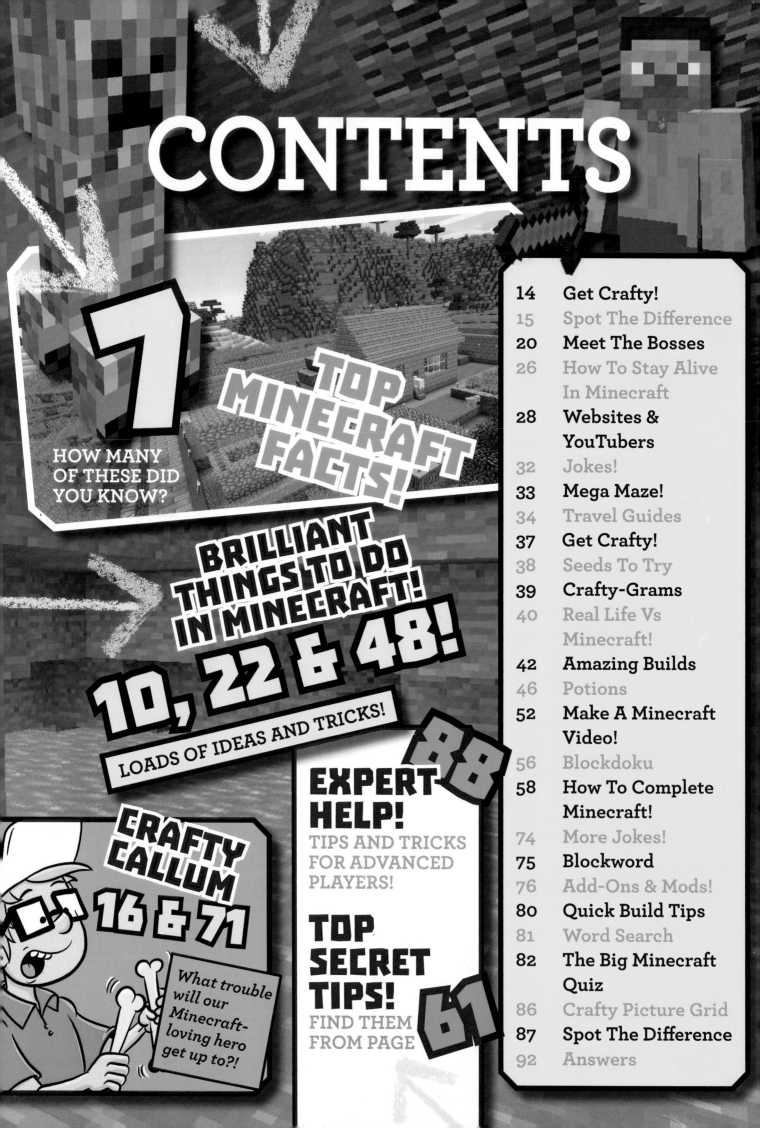

7

TOP MINECRAFT FACTS!

HOW MANY OF THESE DID YOU KNOW?

BRILLIANT THINGS TO DO IN MINECRAFT!

10, 22 & 48!

LOADS OF IDEAS AND TRICKS!

CRAFTY CALLUM

16 & 71

What trouble will our Minecraft-loving hero get up to?!

EXPERT HELP!

88

TIPS AND TRICKS FOR ADVANCED PLAYERS!

TOP SECRET TIPS!

FIND THEM FROM PAGE

61

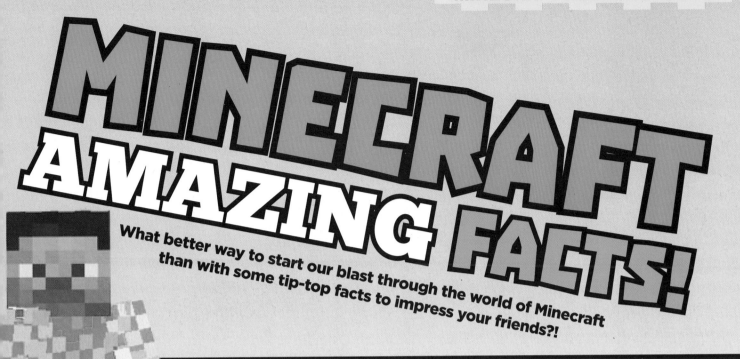

MINECRAFT AMAZING FACTS!

What better way to start our blast through the world of Minecraft than with some tip-top facts to impress your friends?!

The first version of Minecraft was officially available at the end of 2011 but, before that, early test versions were available as far back as May 2009!

The very first version of Minecraft, created by Markus Persson (aka Notch), took just six days to get into a playable state!

The music in Minecraft is done by a man called C418, whose real name is Daniel Rosenfeld. He's released official soundtrack albums too, if you want to listen to Minecraft even when you're not playing the game!

The company behind Minecraft, Mojang, was bought by Microsoft (the company who made Windows) in a mega deal back in the autumn of 2014. Microsoft paid $2.5bn for Mojang – and that was just so it could get its hands on Minecraft!

The original name for Minecraft was actually a lot more simple – it was just called Cave Game! Then it became Minecraft: Order Of The Stone, before being shortened to just Minecraft.

The game has its own mysterious ghost – Herobrine! It's claimed that Herobrine – a Steve-like figure with very different eyes! – occasionally appears in the game, with many people reckoning they've seen him. Thing is, despite the Minecraft team making occasional jokey references to him, he doesn't actually exist!

The first official spin-off game series, Minecraft: Story Mode, was released in 2015. The many episodes released since have taken characters through lots of adventures in the Minecraft world!

Within a month of officially being made available, Minecraft sold a million copies! What made this even more incredible was that Mojang hadn't bought any ads to promote the game – its success was down to people telling each other about it!

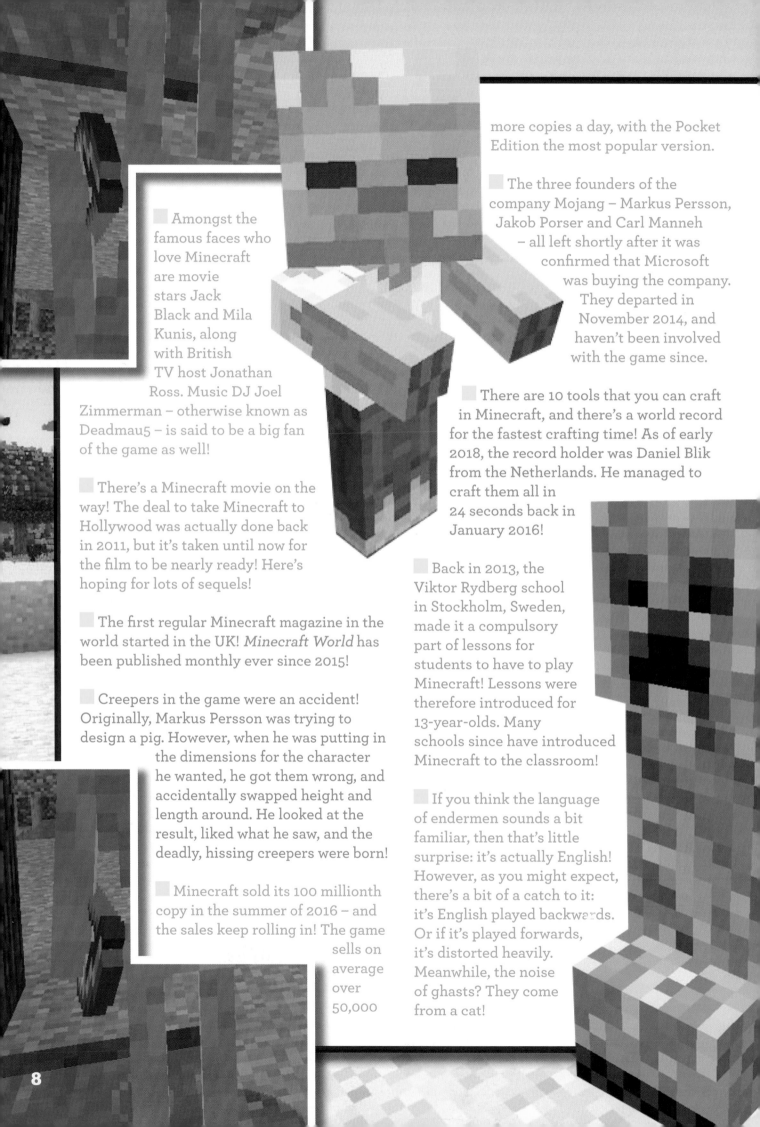

Amongst the famous faces who love Minecraft are movie stars Jack Black and Mila Kunis, along with British TV host Jonathan Ross. Music DJ Joel Zimmerman – otherwise known as Deadmau5 – is said to be a big fan of the game as well!

There's a Minecraft movie on the way! The deal to take Minecraft to Hollywood was actually done back in 2011, but it's taken until now for the film to be nearly ready! Here's hoping for lots of sequels!

The first regular Minecraft magazine in the world started in the UK! *Minecraft World* has been published monthly ever since 2015!

Creepers in the game were an accident! Originally, Markus Persson was trying to design a pig. However, when he was putting in the dimensions for the character he wanted, he got them wrong, and accidentally swapped height and length around. He looked at the result, liked what he saw, and the deadly, hissing creepers were born!

Minecraft sold its 100 millionth copy in the summer of 2016 – and the sales keep rolling in! The game sells on average over 50,000 more copies a day, with the Pocket Edition the most popular version.

The three founders of the company Mojang – Markus Persson, Jakob Porser and Carl Manneh – all left shortly after it was confirmed that Microsoft was buying the company. They departed in November 2014, and haven't been involved with the game since.

There are 10 tools that you can craft in Minecraft, and there's a world record for the fastest crafting time! As of early 2018, the record holder was Daniel Blik from the Netherlands. He managed to craft them all in 24 seconds back in January 2016!

Back in 2013, the Viktor Rydberg school in Stockholm, Sweden, made it a compulsory part of lessons for students to have to play Minecraft! Lessons were therefore introduced for 13-year-olds. Many schools since have introduced Minecraft to the classroom!

If you think the language of endermen sounds a bit familiar, then that's little surprise: it's actually English! However, as you might expect, there's a bit of a catch to it: it's English played backwards. Or if it's played forwards, it's distorted heavily. Meanwhile, the noise of ghasts? They come from a cat!

Apparently, one in every 10,000 times that you play the game, the title of Minecraft will be spelt incorrectly on the opening screen! Instead of Minecraft, it will read Minceraft!

Markus Persson was part-inspired to write Minecraft thanks to a couple of games he loved to play: Rollercoaster Tycoon and Dungeon Keeper. The first tasked you with building a theme park with incredible rollercoasters. The second saw you as a dungeon master trying to defeat the adventurers within.

Unlike many games of its time, Minecraft's gestation and development was recorded as it was happening! A regular blog kept fans of the game up to date with new features and ideas, and it's something many companies now do as a matter of course. Not for the first time, Minecraft was ahead of the crowd!

One bug in the game remained for several years before anybody noticed it! It was confirmed in a post on the Minecraft website, where developer Michael Stoyke admitted that he'd made an error in the game's world generator, which could lead to the whole world being flipped. He mixed up two coordinates, and nobody seemed to notice for nearly three years!

In 2017, over 50 billion views of Minecraft videos were recorded around the world, with services such as YouTube leading the way. It's estimated that over five BILLION hours of Minecraft videos were watched on YouTube alone in 2017!

Over half of all children aged 9-11 in America have played Minecraft – but also in America, Mojang revealed that the average age of the Minecraft player is 24!

Minecraft is the best-selling game of all time on the PC platform, with sales more than doubling those of titles such as The Sims and Myst. Not bad for a game that's never had a sequel or anything!

101 THINGS TO DO

PART 1

In Minecraft, you can do whatever your imagination allows, but sometimes we all need a helping hand. If you're looking for ideas, pick a random number off this list to cross off!

1 Add streetlights along the paths in every village so mobs never spawn there. Not only will it make the village easier to spot, it will help keep the villagers safe! Don't forget to light inside the houses too.

2 Craft a resource block for every type of valuable material: iron, gold, diamond and emerald. You need at least nine ingots or gems to craft a single resource block.

3 Craft several slime blocks, position them a few blocks apart, and try to bounce between them without hitting the ground! If you take damage, start again.

4 Craft a colour palette by creating one of each of the 16 colours of terracotta, stained glass, concrete and wool.

5 Try and craft a banner that looks like your favourite real-life flag! Banners can have up to six layers and tonnes of patterns, so can get complicated!

6 Build a portal to the Nether, walk as far as you can manage in one direction, build a portal back to the Overworld, then see if you can walk back to your base! Bonus points if you don't use a compass.

7 Craft a secret door using pistons and a lever. Remember to disguise the lever. Use bookcases or stone bricks for the door so it can blend into a wall.

Villages are dangerous at night!

Gold blocks can be used for beacons

Craft banners that look like real flags

8 Enchant books until you have one of every kind of enchantment to use. In the Java Edition, there are at least 34 enchantments to collect. (Don't worry about the level of the enchantments!)

9 Grow a tree in a cave – you'll have to dig out enough space, make sure there's good lighting, and bring dirt to plant the sapling. Use bonemeal to speed it up!

10 Collect every type of single-block flower and then plant them in a plant pot. There are 10 in total: dandelion, poppy, blue orchid, allium, azure bluet, oxeye daisy, and then red, orange, white and pink tulips.

11 Craft a glowstone block without visiting the Nether. You'll have to go hunting for witches, but they'll eventually drop enough glowstone dust for you to put together one of the blocks.

12 Build a stone circle in the middle of a grass plain, just like Stonehenge! If you build it big enough, you can plant a tree or create an altar in the middle.

13 Automate the doors in your base using pressure plates. Just remember not to put them outside, otherwise mobs will be able to get in when they approach your door.

14 Find a village and move into one of the houses. Extend it, decorate the interior, dig a basement or add a second floor – there are loads of ways to customise it.

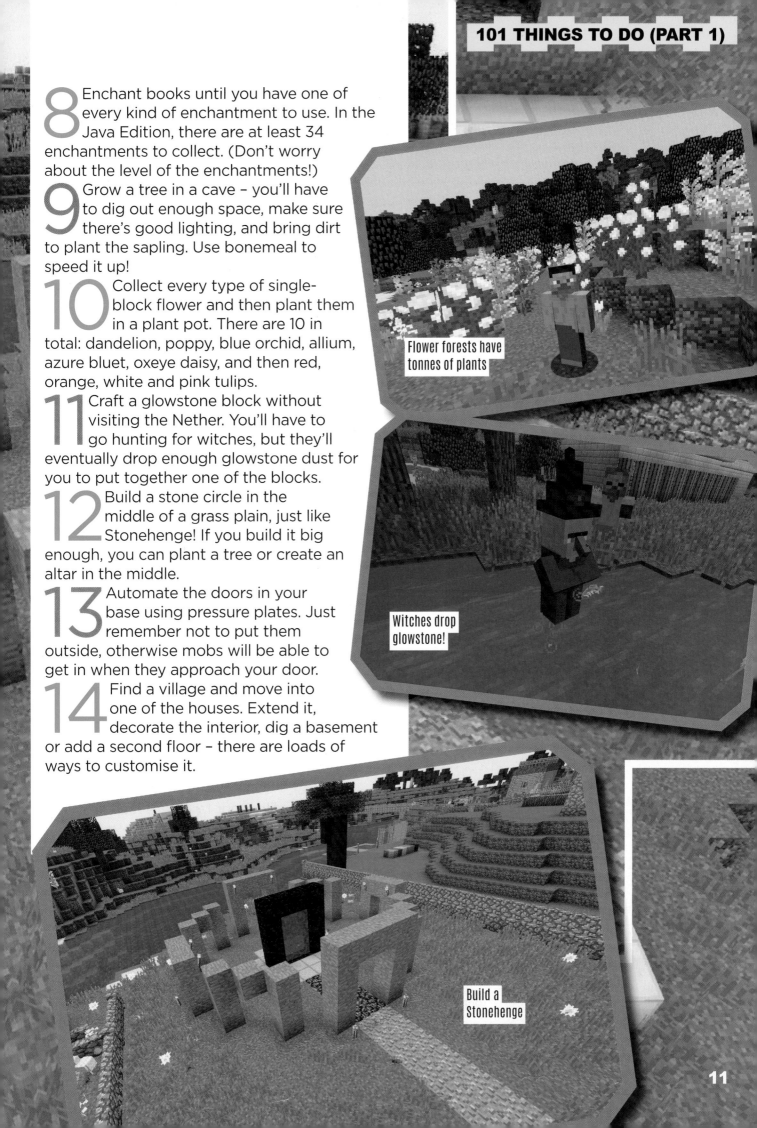

Flower forests have tonnes of plants

Witches drop glowstone!

Build a Stonehenge

Can you dry out a monument?

Make a solid gold throne

Protect a village with a wall

15 Wall off an ocean stronghold and then dry it out completely. This will take a LONG time, but it's very cool once you manage it because you basically have a free castle!

16 Most houses in a village have little to no furniture, so why not make things more homely for everyone by adding furniture to all of the homes in a village?

17 Build yourself a throne out of solid gold blocks, then place it in a throne room so you can rule over your Minecraft land!

18 Collect name tags and use them to give all the villagers in a village names. You can create whole families, or take the names of characters from your favourite film or TV show!

19 Cure a zombie villager to turn it back into a villager. You need to hit it with a splash Potion of Weakness and then feed it an enchanted golden apple.

20 Build a defensive wall around a village to keep the inhabitants safe from mobs at night. If you line the walls with cacti, they'll injure mobs that get too close!

21 Create a small farm where you can grow every type of crop: wheat, potatoes, carrots, pumpkins, melons, cocoa pods, sugar cane and beetroot.

22 Where mobs have different skins, collect one of each type. There are three cat skins (plus the ocelot) and six types of rabbit. There are 34 horse variants though, so maybe just go for one of each colour then instead!

23 Play the game as a mole-man: build an underground base and then stay underground except at night. To play this challenge, you're never allowed out in normal daylight.

24 Shear a mooshroom so that it turns into a normal cow.

25 See how long you can survive in Hardcore mode. Remember, death in Hardcore is permanent, so don't get TOO creative.

26 Build a mine entrance into your base so that you can get underground without leaving the safety of your home. Take care not to let mobs in – seal it with a metal door.

27 Plant a garden with one of every type of tree: oak, spruce, birch, jungle tree, acacia and dark oak. Remember to plant the giant versions of spruce and jungle tree too!

28 Play the game as a nomad: never sleep in the same place twice. Carry your bed with you and pull it up every morning as you head off in a new direction!

29 Build a bridge over a river using lilypads. Just remember, if you crash a boat into the lilypads, they'll break and sink, so build it somewhere you don't need to sail!

30 Empty out a jungle or desert temple and then use it as your new base. You'll need to deactivate the traps and add lighting.

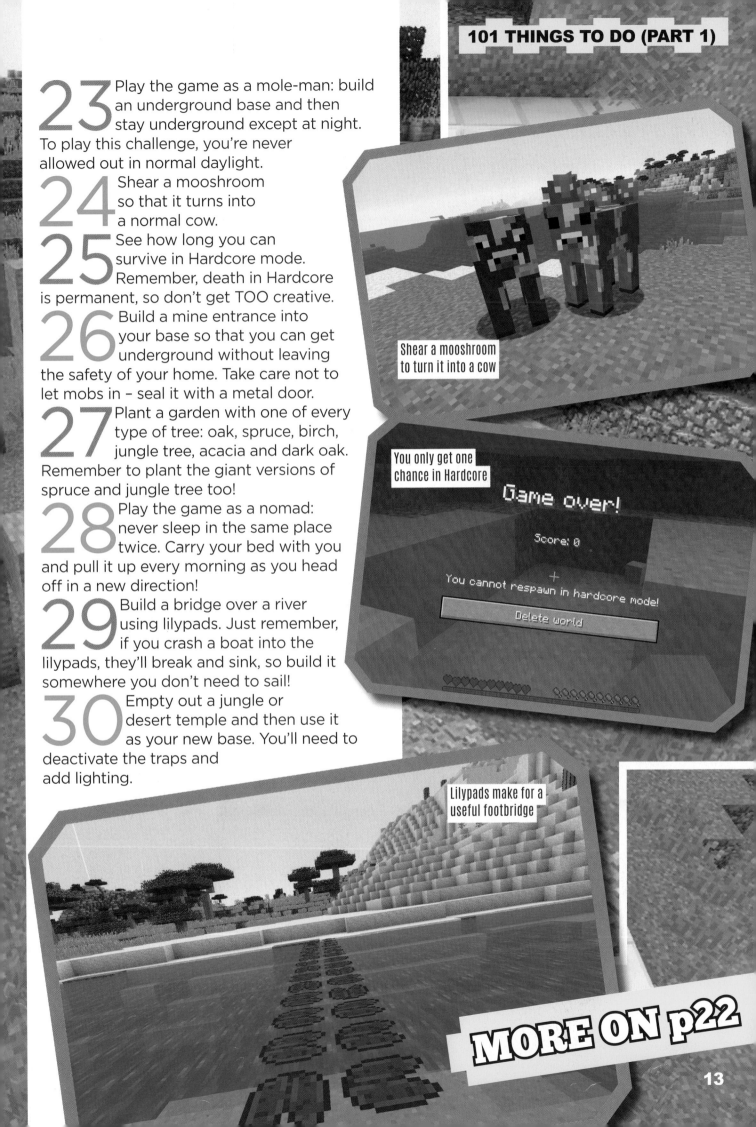

Shear a mooshroom to turn it into a cow

You only get one chance in Hardcore

Game over!

Score: 0

You cannot respawn in hardcore mode!

Delete world

Lilypads make for a useful footbridge

MORE ON p22

GET CRAFTY!

It's time to get creative!
Have fun colouring in this wither! Try and make it look as much like the game as you can or choose a different look – it's up to you!

What do you think would be the perfect background for this picture?

SPOT-THE-DIFFERENCE

We've made seven sneaky changes to the second picture – can you spot them?

15

16

MEET & BEAT THE BOSSES

If you think endermen are hard to kill, just wait until you encounter some of Minecraft's bosses! But who are these deadliest foes, where can you find them, and how do you beat them?

THE ENDER DRAGON

There's only one ender dragon in every Minecraft world, and it spawns naturally in the End. This powerful foe is kept alive by a network of magical End crystals, which replenish its health as it guards the central island of the End and the cities beyond.

Defeating the ender dragon is tough, but it can be done. First, you need to destroy the ender crystals while dodging its attacks – a bow and arrow is the fastest way to do that. Next, attack the dragon when it swoops low, either with a sword or arrows. The secret is to learn its attack patterns, and know when to dodge and when to attack. Keep at it!

If you defeat the ender dragon, you get 12,000 (twelve THOUSAND!) experience points and the exit portal activates, allowing you to return to the Overworld. It also leaves behind a dragon egg.

Destroy crystals to harm the ender dragon.

THE WITHER

Summoned by the dark energy unleashed by combining three wither skeleton skulls with soul sand, the wither is a terrifying force. Its explosive skulls inflict the deadly Wither effect on you, and it takes out EVERYTHING living, so don't summon one unless you want a real challenge!

What can you see?

Build this to summon the wither

Elder guardians guard some gold

To defeat the wither, you need a powerful sword and armour. Attack quickly with enchanted weapons, and don't stop until it dies! Try and summon it underground – if it makes it out to open sky, you'll never get close enough to attack.

Kill the wither, and you'll collect 50 experience points and a Nether star, which allows you to craft beacon blocks. You can summon a wither every time you have enough skulls, and you'll get a wither star every time you defeat one.

ELDER GUARDIANS

Living underwater, elder guardians inhabit the strange ocean monuments that appear in the deepest oceans. While there can be several in each monument, there's always one inside the treasure room. Huge, powerful and with a status effect that actively stops you escaping,

they might be the hardest boss in the game!

To fight an elder guardian, make sure you build a wall of blocks to hide behind when it attacks with its lasers. Take a sword or a trident, and bring plenty of milk to cure the Mining Fatigue. Don't forget to set up an air pocket before you start, otherwise you'll end up with a lungful of water!

Defeat an elder guardian, and you'll get 10 experience, some prismarine shards or crystals, a sponge, as well as a raw fish.

101 THINGS TO DO

Looking for more ways to kill time in your Minecraft world? In the absence of any in-game quests, we've compiled a list of stuff you can do just because we think it's fun!

31 Collect every type of weed: grass, ferns, dead bushes, vines and lilypads. Plant them in your garden to form an artificial copse.

32 Give mobs one of the following names using a name tag: call a rabbit "Toast", a sheep "jeb_" and ANY mob "dinnerbone" or "grumm", and then see what happens.

33 Create a wall clock by putting a regular clock inside an item frame. The perfect timepiece – at least until Minecraft adds smart watches!

34 Dye sheep so that you've got one of each colour! There can be up to 16 – one for every colour of dye, including white.

Make a wall clock

Dyed sheep

It's just a statue!

35 Build a Nether portal without mining any obsidian by using buckets of water and buckets of lava to create obsidian in the shape of a portal and then activating it.

36 Build a giant statue of a mob using concrete, wool, or some other coloured block. We went for pig, but if you're feeling REALLY adventurous, try Steve or Alex!

37 Tame a donkey and a horse, and then use them to breed a mule. You'll have to feed them sugar to put them in breeding mode.

38 Catch one of every type of fish. You can get cod, salmon, clownfish and pufferfish, though some of these are very rare! Try not to eat them TOO quickly...!

39 Map out the local area around your base and then put the maps in item frames on the wall. You can tile them together to make bigger-looking maps.

40 Build a moat around your base and then fill it with water. If you're feeling up for a REAL challenge, create a retractable moat using pistons.

41 Build an art gallery in your base where you have one of each type of painting. You'll have to get creative to make sure the gaps on the wall are the right size.

42 Make a zoo with every type of animal mob. You'll need spiders, polar bears, sheep, cows, pigs, llamas, rabbits, horses, donkeys, mules, wolves, turtles, chickens, ocelots and mooshrooms. Give each one a pen and landscape it!

43 Blow up a creeper on purpose by lighting it with a flint and steel! Just remember to back away quickly so you don't get hurt.

44 Make a maze in your garden. You can build it out of leaf blocks (to resemble bushes!) or stone. Don't forget to put something cool at the centre!

45 Empty a stronghold library of its books so that you never have to craft one again! You might need to make several trips to collect all that reading material.

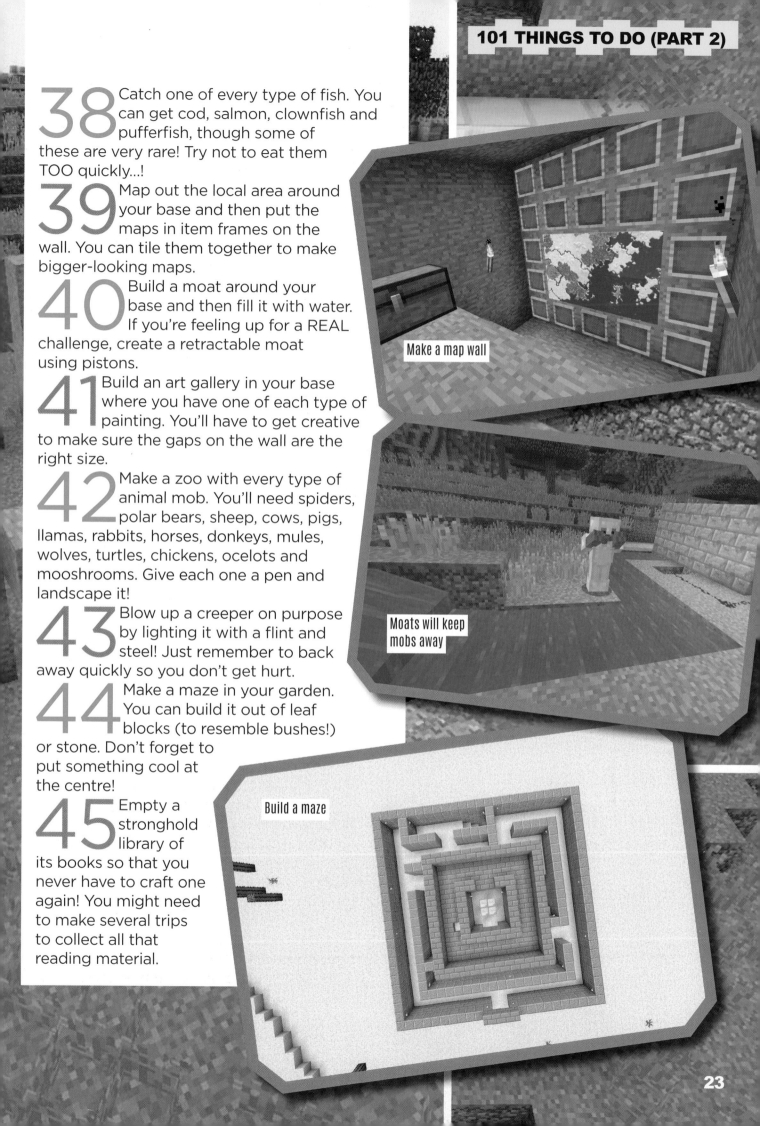

Make a map wall

Moats will keep mobs away

Build a maze

46 Build a secondary base underground so that you don't have to return to the surface while exploring underground. Make sure it's nice and secure though – mobs WILL come for you.

47 Defeat a jungle temple without setting off the traps or breaking any blocks. Harder than it looks, especially if you've never properly beaten a temple before.

48 Find a witch's hut and steal the cauldron from inside it! You can't find cauldrons anywhere else in the game.

49 Collect every music disc and create a jukebox to play them on. There are 12 tracks in total, though one (called "11") is the unsettling shattered record.

50 Build an underground farm so that you've got a ready food supply when exploring. All it takes is dirt, water and light, just like it does above ground.

51 Find a small village and start to expand it with new houses until more villagers spawn there. Buildings must have doors to spawn a new villager.

52 Try making a living as a fisherman (or woman) – only use food and items you pull out of the water with your rod. Be prepared to spend a lot of time waiting on the banks of rivers and lakes...

53 Create themed buildings, like a fast food diner or shop, so that you can invite friendly players into your world and role-play with them inside your creation.

Watch out for traps!

Collect music discs by making these guys fight

Get fishing!

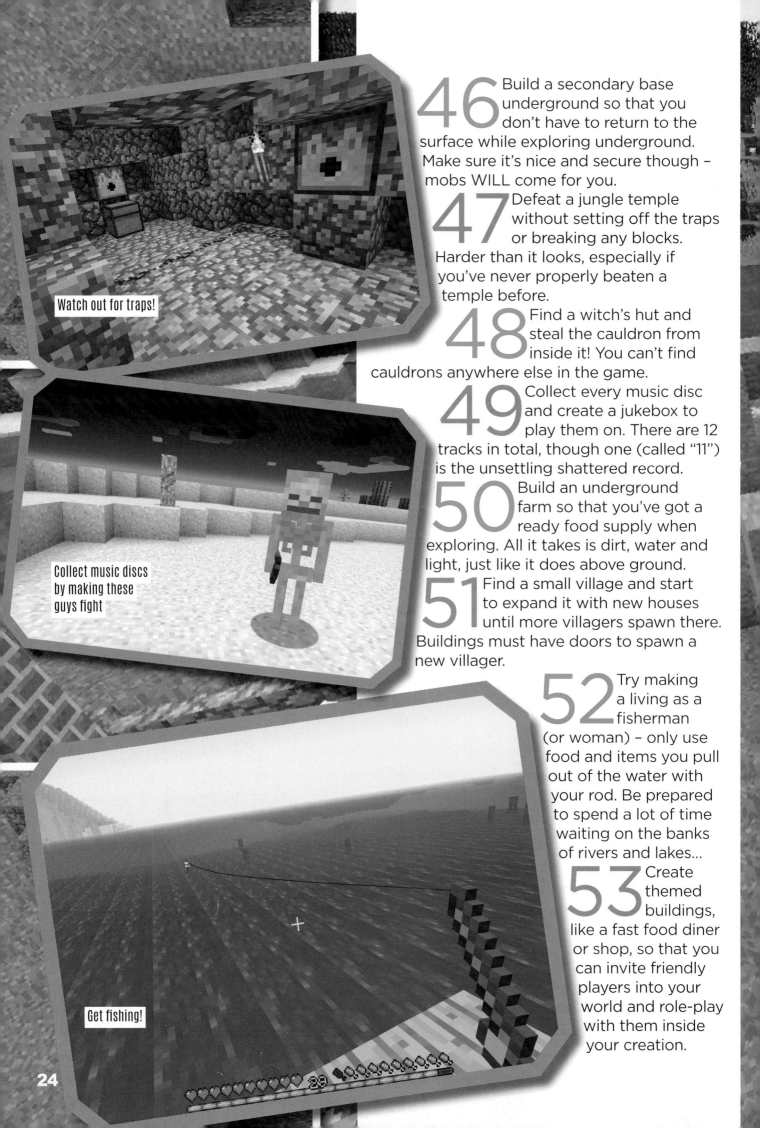

54 Use a book and quill to keep a diary of your adventures so that you can save it for later. Don't finalise the book until it's full – and remember to make a copy once you're done to avoid severe disappointment.

55 Build the walls of a bunker out of pure obsidian so that not even the most determined creeper can leave a scratch on it.

56 Set off in a boat and look for an island that has no trees or food on it, then try to make it a sustainable place to live with resources. Take saplings and seeds with you!

57 Landscape a village with features like fountains and archways so that it looks more welcoming. Perhaps add a park with benches and a pond? Adding decoration makes any location more fun.

58 Dye some leather clothing so that you can mix and match any colour! Clothes can be made in literally thousands of colours if you dye and then re-dye them.

59 Experiment with different firework stars to create your own unique firework style, then set off several together for a cool fireworks display.

60 Use a saddle on a pig and, instead of controlling it with a carrot on a stick, let it wander and see where it takes you. Who knows what weird adventures you'll have together?

Page 1 of 1

Write whatever you like here!_

Sign   Done

Record your adventures in a book

Set off in a boat!

Saddle a pig

MORE ON p48

STAYING ALIVE

Minecraft's world might seem like a friendly place, but something's always trying to finish you off! So if you want to keep on crafting day after day, here are some essential tips for staying alive.

■ ALWAYS CARRY FOOD

Keeping your hunger bar full will replenish your health, making you harder to kill. Cooked steak and porkchops restore 8 points of health and 12.8 points of saturation, making them the best food for survival. Most importantly, they stack in the inventory so you can carry a lot at once!

■ DON'T RUN TOO QUICKLY

Running makes your hunger bar drop very quickly, and when your hunger's low it can start affecting your health. That means you should only run in emergencies – to get places fast, tame a horse or use a boat. Only run from mobs!

■ THE BEST DEFENCE...

One way to stay alive is to make sure nothing else does. Use extra-damaging critical hits in combat: with a sword or axe, jump and strike your enemy as you land. With a bow or trident, charge it as much as possible before attacking.

■ GET SOME REST

Unless you're specifically looking for mob drops, the smartest way to survive is to not fight at all. Carry a bed with you and sleep in it to skip nights before the mobs come out. Just remember that if you die and the bed you slept in is no longer there, you'll restart at your original spawn point!

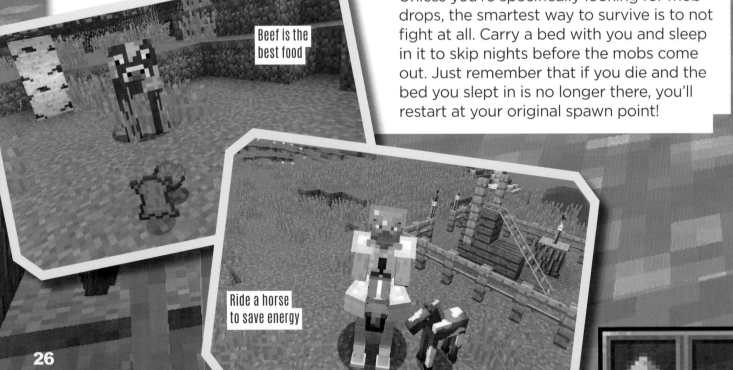

Beef is the best food

Ride a horse to save energy

Critical hits do more damage

A full moon means stronger enemies

■ STOCK UP ON THE ESSENTIALS

The most useful blocks in the game are cobblestone, wood planks and iron ingots – they appear in around 100 different crafting recipes between them. With these three items you can make all of the essential ones, from furnaces and crafting tables to tools, weapons and armour. Don't leave home without them!

■ KEEP AN EYE ON THE MOON

Sometimes you have to go out at night, but in that case why not make it the easier nights? A full moon makes mobs more likely to spawn with bonus status effects and high-level equipment. Stay indoors if the moon is full!

■ STAY AWAY FROM LAVA

Burning to death is no fun, but that goes double if you drown in lava and it incinerates all the stuff you drop as well. If you have to approach lava, hold down the sneak button to try and stop yourself falling in.

■ TAME SOME WOLVES

If you're planning to go out fighting, a tame wolf is an essential ally to have around. Not only will they chase skeletons away and go after mobs you might not have seen yet, but some mobs – like endermen – don't even spot them coming.

■ PUT TORCHES EVERYWHERE

Light keeps hostile mobs from spawning and draws friendly mobs in. You can never have too many torches around. They're also handy if you want to find your way back from a long journey once night hits!

Wolves will fight your battles

Lava incinerates your stuff as well as you!

25 ESSENTIAL MINECRAFT WEBSITES

The best thing about Minecraft is that the community is huge. Check out these websites to learn more about your favourite game and what other people are doing with it!

REMEMBER TO GET YOUR GROWN-UP'S PERMISSION BEFORE VISITING ANY WEBSITES!

ESSENTIAL SITES FOR EVERYONE

■ Official Minecraft Site
minecraft.net
The official home of Minecraft. Get news updates, buy the Java Edition, log in and change your skin.

■ Minecraft Wiki
minecraft.gamepedia.com
The online encyclopaedia that houses information about everything Minecraft has – or has ever had – inside it.

■ Minecraft Forum
www.minecraftforum.net
Whether you need help with a problem or want to share something you've done with other players, this is the place!

■ Official Minecraft Twitter
twitter.com/Minecraft
Want the LATEST news and updates? The official Minecraft Twitter account is always worth looking at for up-to-the-minute news.

■ Minecraft Twitch
www.twitch.tv/directory/game/Minecraft
If you can't play Minecraft, why not watch other people doing it in real time on the Twitch streaming network?!

■ The Skindex
www.minecraftskins.com
If you want to customise the look of your character, The Skindex is the place to go, with thousands of skins and instructions on getting them all into the game.

■ Minecraft: Story Mode
telltale.com/series/minecraft-story-mode
It's Minecraft, but not as you know it! You can learn all Story Mode on the official Telltale Games website.

Minecraft.net

Minecraft Twitch

Skindex

ESSENTIAL SITES FOR BEDROCK (POCKET/ WINDOWS 10) EDITION PLAYERS

■ Minecraft PE Downloads

mcpedl.com

The top website for Minecraft Bedrock Edition mods, maps, skins, seeds and texture packs, all easily accessible with descriptions and screenshots. Whatever you want to do with the Bedrock Edition, this place has the content you need.

■ Minecraft PE Wiki

minecraftpocketedition.wikia.com

If you only play the Bedrock Edition, this Wiki is the best choice – you won't get confused by Console or Java Edition behaviour because this is 100% Pocket/ Windows 10 Edition from the ground up. Great for learning what everything does.

■ Minecraft Pocket Edition Servers

minecraftpocket-servers.com

Do you want to play Minecraft online? Of course you do! But finding servers can be hard, so why not try picking them from this online list of popular servers. It even shows you how many people are playing on them and allows you to search their database!

■ Tynker

www.tynker.com

Aimed at kids who want to code, Tynker has its own Minecraft-specific section that will teach you how to make a skin, create an Add-On, or mod specific new items into the game. Great fun!

■ MCPE Files

mcpefl.com

Nothing but Add-Ons and texture packs here, all for the Bedrock Edition. You'll find everything from new items to complete sub-games to try out. Don't miss it!

■ r/MCPE

www.reddit.com/r/MCPE

Reddit's Minecraft Pocket Edition forum – covering the Bedrock Edition, obviously – has all the best links and discussions on this edition of Minecraft.

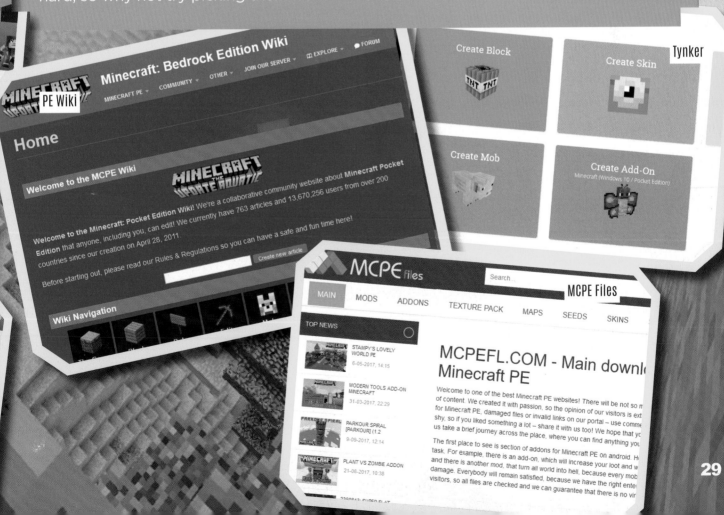

ESSENTIAL SITES FOR JAVA (PC) EDITION PLAYERS

■ Minecraft Seed HQ
minecraftseedhq.com
Whatever type of map you want to play on, you'll be able to find it at the Minecraft Seed HQ alongside all sorts of interesting and weird seeds. They've got an archive of content that covers almost every version of the game, so you'll never get bored!

■ Minecraft Maps
minecraftmaps.com
Fancy checking out someone else's Minecraft world rather than building your own? The Minecraft Maps website is the biggest and best repository of maps and mini-game downloads. Just make sure you know how to use them safely!

■ Forge
www.minecraftforge.net
Downloading mods is fine, but if you want to install them then there's one place you need to go, and that's the Forge website. You have to download and install Forge before you can play any mods, so don't waste time – go get it!

■ MinecraftSix
minecraftsix.com
Another online repository of downloadable content for the Java Edition, including mods, maps, resource packs, texture packs and tools. Everything a PC player could want!

■ Planet Minecraft
planetminecraft.com
Part of the popular Planet network, this site has perhaps more content than any other – everything from skins and texture packs, to server lists and projects to view. A great place for beginners to start experiencing Minecraft!

■ Minecraft World Map
www.minecraftworldmap.com
This map-focused site lets you preview worlds in fantastic detail before you decide whether to install and play them. It's almost worth uploading stuff just to use the awesome 3D map explorer!

ESSENTIAL YOUTUBERS

■ CaptainSparklez

tinyurl.com/mw-sparklez

With 10 million subscribers, CaptainSparklez is one of the biggest Minecraft YouTubers, and that's probably because he makes his own music videos! You can watch them for free on his channel, and also buy them on iTunes.

■ Amy Lee

tinyurl.com/mw-amylee

Amy Lee's channel is mainly aimed at girls, and posts at least one new video every day! There are lots of series which go up every week, including Crazy Craft, and her own series, Amy's Land of Love.

■ Preston Playz

tinyurl.com/mw-prestonplayz

Built off the popularity of his awesome parkour map runs, Preston Playz now has loads of Minecraft videos up to view. He also does his best to highlight fan-generated content, and some super interesting things like droppers, unfair maps and glitch videos.

■ DanTDM

tinyurl.com/mw-danTDM

The richest UK YouTuber of 2017, DanTDM has over 17 million subscribers. His Minecraft survival mod videos and mini-game showcases are great ways to see some cool versions of Minecraft you might never have played before!

■ Little Kelly Minecraft

tinyurl.com/mw-littlekelly

Little Kelly is a kid-friendly channel from Ireland which adds new videos almost every day. The videos are good fun for anyone, but especially girls! Little Kelly is part of a group called "The Little Club" which includes loads of other channels you can watch!

■ Sqaishey Quack

tinyurl.com/mw-sqaishey

A kid-friendly channel following the adventures of a bright yellow duck. Great for younger players! A new video goes up most days, and you can watch tonnes of stuff, including a great attempt to play in Hardcore mode!

WHICH STAR WARS FILM DO MINECRAFT MOBS LOVE THE MOST?
PHANTOM MENACE!

WHY WERE THE CREEPERS BANNED FROM PARTIES?
THEY KEPT BLOWING UP BALLOONS!

WHAT DID ALEX DO WHEN STEVE ANNOYED HER ON SOCIAL MEDIA?
SHE BLOCKED HIM!

WHY DID THE ENDER DRAGON ALWAYS STRUGGLE WITH STORIES?
HE ALWAYS WENT STRAIGHT TO THE END!

MINECRAFT JOKES!

DID YOU HEAR ABOUT THE WITCH WHO WENT TO THE HAIRDRESSERS?
SHE HAD A SCARE CUT!

WHY DID STEVE STRUGGLE TO GET TO SLEEP?
BECAUSE OF THE BEDROCK!

WHY COULDN'T THE CREEPER RECOGNISE STEVE?
HE'D JUST JUMPED OUT OF HIS SKIN!

MEGA MAZE!

Welcome intrepid adventurer! Can you find your way to the centre of this mega axe maze and retrieve the golden axe? If you could, it would be a-maze-ing! Start here... Good luck!

33

TRAVEL GUIDE –
THE NETHER

Sick of getting rained on in the Overworld? Why not try out the Nether, where the weather's always scorching – and if you don't believe us, try taking a dip in one of the many lava pools. You'll soon change your mind!

NETHER SAY NETHER AGAIN

Made out of strange, permanently burning netherrack and filled with the scariest mobs around, the Nether is a perfect place to test yourself against the worst Minecraft has to offer. Don't worry if your first trip ends in disaster – just come back with more armour and a stronger weapon.

HAPPY FORTS

Up for a challenge? The Nether is home to the huge Nether fortresses, which are packed with strong mobs and full of loot, not to mention the best source of nether wart, a vital ingredient in potions, and blaze powder, which helps you brew.

SHORTCUT

The Nether isn't just a weird place to visit – you can also use it to make shortcuts through the Overworld. Every step you take here is worth eight in the Overworld, so build a portal in the Nether and pop back to the Overworld to see where you've ended up. Chances are it will be somewhere completely unexplored!

And best of all, a trip to or from the Nether takes just seconds because it's always only one portal ride away.

The terrifying Nether

Nether fortresses are massive

A portal back to the Overworld

Southern Meadow

TRAVEL GUIDE – THE END

Think the Overworld is SO over? Are you never going back to the Nether? Well, there's one place that only the smartest, strongest and bravest can reach, and that's the End – home of the terrifying endermen and the infamous ender dragon. Only seasoned adventurers need apply!

DRAGON PUNCH

Before you can see the impressive End cities and glide your way home with a pair of elytra, you'll need to defeat the huge and powerful ender dragon. Bring a friend! Bring three or four! Because this dragon won't go down without a fight.

END OF THE ROAD

Composed of large islands in a floating void, the End is a dimension unlike any other. Just getting from one place to the next involves some serious skill, and with endermen everywhere you shouldn't expect an easy journey. Make it off the central island, and you'll find lots to explore. But there's only one way in and out of the End, so however far you go, you'll have to come the same distance home.

PURPUR REIGN

The End has just one form of plant life and you'll find it everywhere: the strange chorus tree, which also grows its own mysterious fruit. You can bake chorus fruits and craft them into purpur blocks, but when eaten raw they teleport you a short distance away. Don't eat too many, though, otherwise you could end up being teleported into the deadly void!

The ender dragon

The End is made up of several islands

End cities are made of purpur

TRAVEL GUIDE – THE OVERWORLD

The Overworld is Minecraft's most popular destination, with gorgeous scenery, thousands of fun activities to try, and enough raw materials to build the home – or, for that matter, the city – of your dreams!

YOUR BIOME AWAY FROM HOME

Whatever you enjoy, the Overworld has you covered! Spend time trekking across rolling deserts, chilling out amongst the strange ice spikes, swinging through the jungle, or taking a dip in the oceans. With over 30 different biomes to explore, you'll never get bored.

CAN YOU DIG IT?

Tired of exploring the surface? Well, the Overworld is full of caves, ravines and tunnels to get your pickaxe into. Look for precious gems like diamonds and emeralds, unearth fossils of mobs long gone, or break into strange underground strongholds. You could get lost down there for days – literally!

GET MOBBED

Nowhere has a wider variety of life than the Overworld. During the days, you can hunt rabbits, sheep and cows for food, swim with turtles and dolphins, or try your hand at taming a horse. At night, brush up on your target practice with skeletons, zombies and witches to fight – not to forget Minecraft's famous creepers!

Truly, with so much to do, the Overworld is a perfect place to establish a permanent home. Just don't forget your sword...

Ice spikes

Underground

A creeper!

GET CRAFTY!

It's time to get creative!
Get colouring, go crazy, do whatever you like. What do you think would be the perfect background for this picture?

37

TEN TOP SEEDS

A good world seed is the basis of a great game of Minecraft. Here are some awesome ones to get you started!

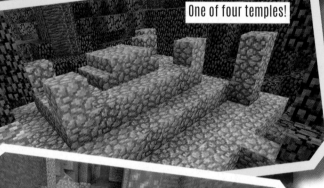

One of four temples!

Mine, all mine

A natural river bridge

Riverside property!

JAVA EDITION SEEDS

093693875598596 If you like jungle temples, this is the seed to use! You'll spawn in a huge jungle that contains four temples in total!

2600835593309946060 Want to get right into the mining part of Minecraft? This seed spawns you by a ravine, and in the bottom is an exposed mine!

53049621178826325538 If you're looking for some cool village variants, this seed puts you right on the edge of a taiga biome that contains a taiga village.

43365071866655949848 This seed puts you by a village that's spawned right on the edge of the coast with some natural piers – and a shipwreck!

1483524782 Most mansions appear far away from spawn points, but this one starts you in a roofed forest with a huge three-storey mansion. Get on top of the trees and look around!

BEDROCK EDITION SEEDS

3259165 If you've never experienced a zombie village, this seed will put you right next to one. Get ready to watch the flames if you start during the day though!

65063 Follow the ravines near this spawn point and you'll see something amazing: a river that crosses over a ravine in a natural bridge.

625444273 Fans of sailing will enjoy this seed, which puts you right on the centre of two rivers that cross!

-518068014 As on the Java Edition, follow the forest and a woodland mansion awaits – this one has its entrance right on a riverside too!

1388582293 This huge settlement might look like a town, but it's actually three villages that have spawned right next to each other!

CRAFTY-GRAMS

HERNET

NAMERDEN

CORDBEK

LAREP

RUPPRU

DEN ICTY

REKHULS

LAPROT

GEG

MOPE

DUNWERLORD

Can you solve these anagrams
and find the words in the green squares?

HINT: It's all about the End!

MINECRAFT
WHICH LOOKS BEST?

What looks better – Minecraft or the real world?! Let's take five famous places and landmarks, and see what you reckon!

REAL

EIFFEL TOWER

Lots of Minecrafters have tried to recreate Paris' most famous landmark – and here's one of the best, from akihirosim!
tinyurl.com/realbuilds2

WEMBLEY STADIUM

REAL

England's football ground plays host to cup finals, international games and concerts. And just look at how it shapes up in Minecraft! Full credit to Minecraft user ITStheMARKEY for this...
tinyurl.com/realbuilds1

Photos: Bigstock

VS REAL LIFE:

REAL

REAL

REAL

STATUE OF LIBERTY

You'll find the Statue Of Liberty in New York over in the USA of course. But you don't have to travel all that way! Just see what player P4wpoz_ managed to put together in Minecraft!
tinyurl.com/realbuilds3

SYDNEY OPERA HOUSE

Let's go to Australia next, to the world famous Sydney Opera House. Save your airfare, though! Just take a look at the Minecraft version done by Avalanche_Ali!
tinyurl.com/realbuilds4

NIAGARA FALLS

Finally, it's one of the most famous waterfalls in the world, and we reckon Minecraft user c4ndyr4vr604 has done a really excellent job here!
tinyurl.com/realbuilds5

REAL

20 AMAZING MINECRAFT BUILDS

Minecraft isn't just about building practical stuff. Over the past few years, players have been making things that are so complicated and dazzling, we bet even the makers of Minecraft wouldn't have thought of them. Here are 20 amazing builds we've discovered on our travels...

UNDERWATER BASE

There are definite downsides to living in a structure under the sea – leaks, drowning and so forth – but this Underwater Base built by Parox is impressive. Its big glass domes offer spectacular views of sea and sky, and the base even has its own farm.

tinyurl.com/ 2019Annual01

2

MECHANICAL ARTHROPOD

Insects, spiders and crustaceans are all arthropods. We doubt you'll find any as big or scary as this robot in a nature book, though. This mechanical arthropod doesn't actually move, which is just fine by us!

tinyurl.com/ 2019Annual02

ULTIMATE SANDCASTLE

The good thing about Minecraft is that you can build huge sandcastles that won't get demolished by the sea. Here's a great example of one: it has turrets, towers, battlements, and even a throne room.

tinyurl.com/ 2019Annual03

1

3

TITAN CITY

Made by art student Duncan Parcells, Titan City is constructed from 4.5 million blocks, and took two years to build. What's more amazing is that he put each block in place by hand, and some of its skyscrapers even have stairs, lifts and furnishings.

tinyurl.com/ 2019Annual04

5 ROBOT

PROGRAMMABLE MINING ROBOT

If you're looking for a loyal robot companion, this one can be programmed to carry out the repetitive task of mining for you. He'll diligently chip away at the rocks, and even extinguish deadly lava with a jet of water. All you have to do is program him, and off he goes. Ingenious!

tinyurl.com/ 2019Annual05

S.H.I.E.L.D HELICARRIER

One of the most memorable ships in the Marvel Cinematic Universe is the gigantic S.H.I.E.L.D Helicarrier, which has been replicated almost perfectly in this build. As well as command decks and engine rooms, it even has a containment cell for the Hulk!

tinyurl.com/ 2019Annual06

6

7

8

LARGE HADRON COLLIDER - WITH CHICKENS

The Large Hadron Collider is dedicated to smashing particles together and examining the results. Here, user spoonmonkeyuk has built a scale replica that smashes chickens together instead. All in the name of science!

tinyurl.com/ 2019Annual7

Chickens create 2 series of waves
All feathers lie at or near a point of intersection
Conclusive proof of dual wave/particle nature of the chicken

NOTE BLOCK WORLD

Here, user you_are_mad has used note blocks to create an entire structure for playing songs. By hitting a switch, a minecart will take you to your selected tune – anything from Adele to Bing Crosby!

tinyurl.com/2019Annual08

9

LUXURY CRUISE SHIP

Holidays on luxury cruise liners aren't everyone's idea of fun, but the detail on this ship is stunning. There are swimming pools, sun loungers, and even places to sit and eat.

tinyurl.com/ 2019Annual09

HOGWARTS

This 1:1 recreation of Hogwarts from Harry Potter is a particularly impressive piece of work. Based on official blueprints from the movies, it's astonishingly accurate, from its great hall to Dumbledore's study and Hagrid's hut.

tinyurl.com/ 2019Annual10

AUTOMATED CHICKEN FARM

What if you freed up some time by creating your own automated chicken farm? A player called Data has built this huge facility where caged chickens lay eggs, which hatch into chicks, which are cooked with lava blocks when fully grown. Disturbing but useful!

tinyurl.com/ 2019Annual11

10

11

13

GIANT BATTLE ROBOT

The most impressive thing about this four-legged monster is you can control it. According to its creator, Cubehamster, the project took around 60 hours to build, and it's also armed with a variety of weapons, including TNT cannons and bomb launchers.

tinyurl.com/2019Annual12

PISTON ELEVATOR

Few lifts are as amazing as this redstone elevator. Capable of sending you to the top of a 14-floor building in seconds, it's equipped with switches and doors that only open when the lift's stopped.

tinyurl.com/ 2019Annual13

PRINTER

Here, you place coloured blocks in a large chest to create a picture, then YouTube user ACtennis AC's printer creates a full-scale version of that image out of large woollen blocks. Superb!

tinyurl.com/ 2019Annual14

12

14

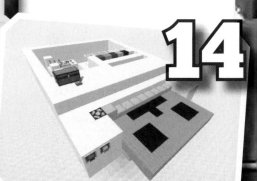

15

DOGFIGHT

FLOATING THEME PARK

Constructed high in the sky, this theme park is unlike any you'll encounter in the real world. It's one of the most striking rollercoasters we've seen.

tinyurl.com/ 2019Annual15

ROCK 'EM SOCK 'EM ROBOTS

Rock 'Em Sock 'Em Robots was popular in the 1960s. It was a two-player fighting game before anybody had computers or consoles. This Minecraft version is complete with working buttons and flying heads.

tinyurl.com/ 2019Annual16

16

GREENFIELD

This city is a seemingly endless sprawl of skyscrapers, residential buildings, shopping precincts and sports stadiums. Suspension bridges take you over the river, you can climb the skyscrapers, or explore the network of underground tunnels.

tinyurl.com/ 2019Annual17

17

AUTOMATIC MINING MACHINE

Looking for a way to dig deep into the earth without all the tiresome shovel work? Then here's a build that's handy as well as fun to watch. At the flick of a switch, the mining machine will use generous dollops of TNT to dig right down to the bedrock – all within a minute or two.

tinyurl.com/ 2019Annual18

18

PRISMATIC MINI-GAME

19

Prismatic presents a series of rooms that must be navigated by manipulating coloured beams of light with glass cubes. It soon becomes a challenging network of interlocking puzzles!

tinyurl.com/ 2019Annual19

INFINITE ROLLERCOASTER GENERATOR

This build lets you create a rollercoaster while sitting in a special diamond minecart – simply press the direction keys to draw the track!

tinyurl.com/ 2019Annual20

20

■ If you don't use nether wart to make an awkward potion, you'll only be able to craft a Potion of Weakness!

■ You need one unit of blaze powder to power about 20 brewing actions. Make sure you have THREE water bottles on a brewing stand whenever you use it, as it takes one blaze powder no matter how many bottles are in there.

■ Remember, potion effects aren't always obvious. Undead mobs are injured by splash Potions of Healing, and healed by splash Potions of Harming!

AWESOME POTION TIPS

Minecraft's potions allow you to power yourself up (or down!) in loads of cool ways. Here's everything you need to know to become a potion master!

■ You can add the following items to an awkward potion to create the following potions:

- Golden carrot = Potion of Night Vision (allows you to see in the dark)
- Magma cream = Potion of Fire Resistance (reduces fire damage)
- Rabbit's foot = Potion of Leaping (increases jump height)

- Sugar = Potion of Swiftness (increases player speed)
- Pufferfish = Potion of Water Breathing (increases breath underwater)
- Glistering melon = Potion of Healing (instantly recovers health)
- Spider eye = Potion of Poison (deals damage)
- Ghast tear = Potion of Regeneration (recovers health over time)
- Blaze powder = Potion of Strength (increases damage dealt by 130%)

Get your nether wart ASAP!

Pufferfish can be added to potions

If you don't have nether wart, add a fermented spider eye (sugar + mushroom + spider eye) to a bottle to make a Potion of Weakness, or gunpowder to make a splash water potion.

If you add any ingredients other than nether wart, fermented spider eye or gunpowder directly to a water bottle, you'll create a useless mundane potion.

Redstone dust extends potions

Kill spiders and use their eyes in potions

Undead mobs are hurt by healing potions

To create stronger/extended potions, you can add redstone, which approximately doubles the time a potion works for, or glowstone, which makes the effect stronger but halves the time it lasts for.

Add gunpowder to make any potion into a splash potion, and add dragon's breath to make a lingering potion.

You can use fermented spider eyes to "corrupt" a potion's effects:
• Potion of Night Vision becomes Potion of Invisibility (causes its target to disappear)
• Potions of Swiftness & Leaping become Potion of Slowness (slows its target)
• Potions of Healing & Poison become Potion of Harming (deals instant damage)

Splash potions allow you to weaken or slow down your enemies, as well as heal and protect allies. Most usefully, a splash potion can affect multiple mobs and players at once as long as they're close to where the potion smashes.

Splash water potions have no effect on mobs that are usually harmed by water, such as blazes and endermen.

101 THINGS TO DO

If you've worked your way through our previous mini-quests, we've got one final batch for you. And if these aren't enough, get a group of friends together and set your own challenges!

61 Make the game harder by avoiding the use of coal and lava in furnaces – the cost of smelting and cooking suddenly becomes a lot more realistic!

62 If you don't like fighting mobs, why not play in Peaceful mode as a "photographer"?

63 Instead of relying on your memory and compass to find your way around, link two villages by building bridges and roads between them.

64 Bring a supply of netherrack, nether quartz, soul sand, purpur blocks and end stone back to the Overworld from their own dimensions.

65 Find a desert temple that's been covered in sand and dig it out like a real archaeologist.

Connect villages with a road

Put netherrack in the Overworld

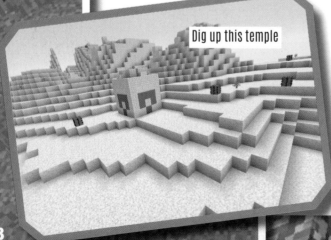

Dig up this temple

66 Enter the Nether, then build a small fortress around the portal to keep yourself safe. Remember not to put a bed in there, though, as it will explode!

67 Become a vegetarian to make it harder (but maybe kinder!) to find food. You'll have to be a lot more careful about what you eat and store.

68 Clear away trees quickly by starting a forest fire. For a challenge, wait until it gets big, then put it out. Bring splash water bottles!

69 Improve a village by replacing the normal paths with stone ones.

70 Scale to the top of the highest savanna plateau mountain you can find without placing or breaking any blocks.

71 You can't farm much in the Nether, but it's possible to grow trees there without water. See if you can make it happen!

72 Bored of regular buildings? Why not collect snow, craft it into blocks and build your own igloo? It shouldn't melt if you build it correctly!

73 Dig all the way down to the bedrock and see what you can find there. Diamonds are quite common, and sometimes you'll even find underground lakes embedded in it!

74 Find a desert well and set up a small trading outpost around it.

75 Sick of getting lost out at sea? Build a tall lighthouse and you'll be able to navigate back.

76 Build a minecart track that passes through a portal to save materials, then ride it.

77 Give your rooms a warm, homely touch by putting in a fireplace. Use netherrack to make it burn like a real fire.

78 Take a cue from the Medieval people by building a farm inside the walls of your castle.

79 Try to survive the game without crafting any torches. Scavenging them is allowed, but maybe not as easy as it sounds!

80 Get all of the achievements/ advancements. What they are (or if you have any!) will vary between platforms, but they should all give you tasks that you might not otherwise think of doing.

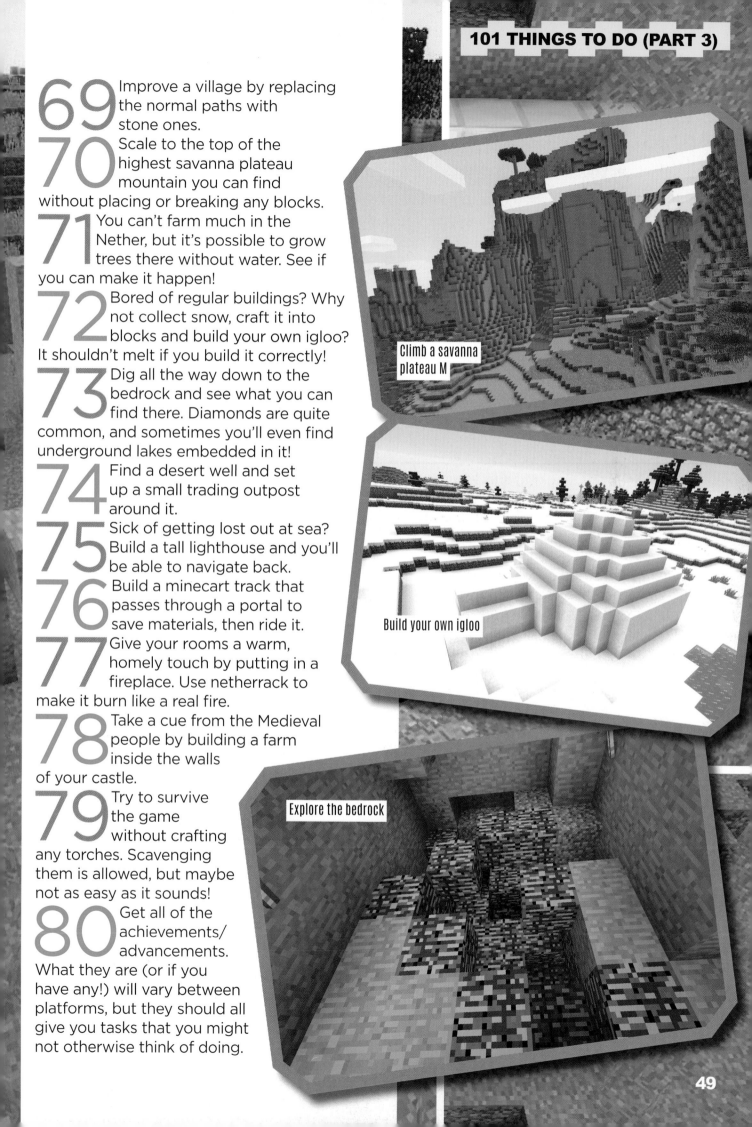

Climb a savanna plateau M

Build your own igloo

Explore the bedrock

81 Use a minecart and rail tracks to create a rollercoaster. You can use triggered rails to make cool things happen when you pass over them!

82 Play the game as a hunter. See how many creepers you can kill in one night (without dying!) and then try to break that record the next night.

83 Minecraft isn't just about exploring and scavenging. You could use coloured blocks like wool and clay to create some pixelart!

84 Create an island sanctuary where every type of tame animal can live freely, safe from wolves and other predators.

85 Instead of crafting items, play a game where you only trade for them. Remember that villagers love emeralds.

86 Find a nice flat area of desert and recreate the sphinx and pyramids to give your world the feel of Ancient Egypt.

87 If you're used to building on the surface or inside caves, why not try building an underwater base? They're hard to make, but very safe – mobs won't get near you!

88 Build a replica of your own house, or another familiar building like your school or a local playground. See how close you can get it!

89 Craft one of each tool in every available material. That means wood, stone, gold, iron and diamond. Display them in item frames to prove you've done it.

90 Build a house of straw, a house of sticks, and a house of bricks. And then, for added fun, put a pig in each one. Just take care in case a wolf shows up!

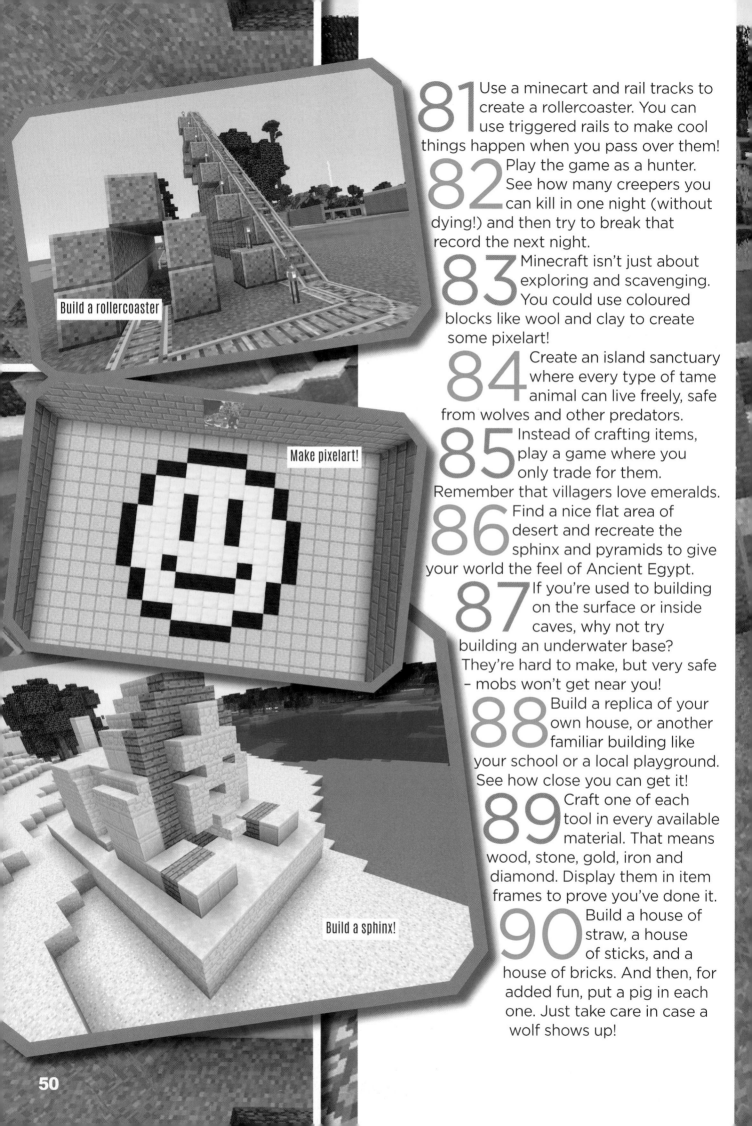

Build a rollercoaster

Make pixelart!

Build a sphinx!

91 You may be handy with a sword, but how well can you survive with only your wits? Why not go hunting at night without any weapons? You can wear armour and take drinkable potions, but nothing else!

92 When you find an abandoned mine, don't leave it until you've discovered the starting room (the one with a dirt floor). Maybe even draw a map of the mine once you know where it starts.

Find the start of a mine and map it

93 Build a beacon out of diamond blocks in Survival mode – or, for a real challenge, emerald blocks!

94 Try to cross a forest without touching the floor. It isn't hard, especially in dense forests, but it gives you a different perspective.

95 Visit the End and kill the ender dragon. Do it with friends, but for a real challenge do it alone!

96 Make your base a treehouse – you can either start somewhere with big enough trees to build on, or plant your own!

Build a diamond beacon in Survival mode

97 Build a spooky graveyard! You can use double chests buried in the ground for coffins, and signs attached to blocks for headstones.

98 Find an abandoned mine and try to repair it. You'll have to reconstruct scaffolding, light it up, and replace the tracks.

99 Try to play the game without crafting ANY furniture – you'll soon learn where to collect rarer things like beds and brewing stands.

100 Create a llama train! You can put carpets on llamas, and there's a different design for each colour of carpet, so try to do all 16!

Make a spooky graveyard

Here Lies Lodark

Urthworm 1982-2016

101 Spawn two withers at the same time, then try and make them fight one another!

HOW TO MAKE A MINECRAFT VIDEO

Recording your games in Minecraft is a great way to show off your creations and share your adventures with other people online. If you're playing on a PC, it's easy to set up!

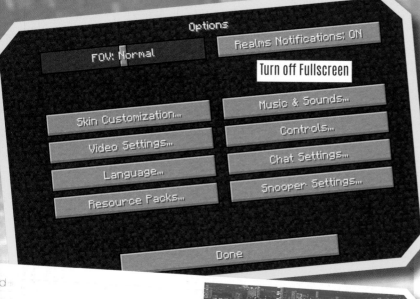

NOTE: Before you run any of the programs mentioned here, you must get the permission of the computer's owner. You may also want their help downloading and installing the programs!

SET UP YOUR SOFTWARE

To record your game of Minecraft, you have to use a screen-recording program. Ezvid for Windows is free to download and use, and the installer can be found on its official site at **www.ezvid.com**

When the installer has downloaded, run it to install the software. An Ezvid icon will appear on your desktop. Open the program and then run Minecraft as normal. Make sure Minecraft isn't running in full-screen mode. If it is, you can change the setting in Minecraft by clicking Options -> Video Settings and turning off Fullscreen.

Place the Minecraft window and the Ezvid windows side-by-side as shown. In the video timeline, right-click on the white frame already in the timeline and

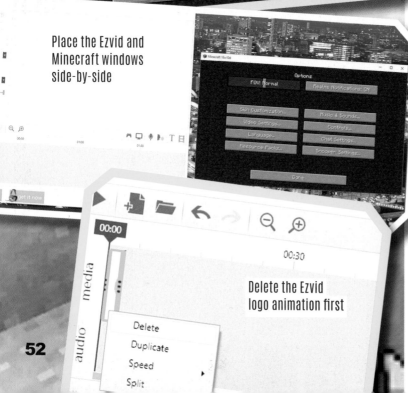

Place the Ezvid and Minecraft windows side-by-side

Delete the Ezvid logo animation first

choose Delete – these are the Ezvid example logos, so you want to get rid of them!

On the left of Ezvid, select a music track. Choose "Silent Machine" if you want to narrate the video yourself, or you can choose your own music from elsewhere. Now click the "Capture Screen" button on the right – it looks like a small computer screen.

At this point, you could click the orange "Start Capture Now" button, but the video would record your entire screen, including the Ezvid window. Instead, click "Use Advanced Settings".

Here's what the advanced settings mean:

If you want to narrate your video as you play, set "Microphone Capture" or "Headset Mode" to "Enabled", depending on which type of mic you have.

The "Select Capture Area" option lets you choose a section of the screen to record. Click this so that it switches to "Enabled".

Finally, if you have a webcam and want the video to show your face while recording, change "Capture Webcam" to "Enabled". We don't recommend this as it will cover up part of the video and slow down the recording.

Beneath the options, you'll see a time limit for your recording in minutes:seconds. The videos will be about 150MB per minute so your system needs lots of free space!

START RECORDING

When you've set your options, click "Start Advanced Capture Now". If you enabled "Select Capture Area", you'll be asked to draw a box around the section of the screen you want to record. Click the left mouse button in the top left of the Minecraft window and hold it down. Drag the cursor to the bottom right and let go. You've now told Ezvid to only record the Minecraft window.

After a short countdown, the recording will begin. A set of video controls will appear so that you can pause/restart or stop the recording, as well as a set of drawing tools to point out certain things to your viewers.

Enable Capture Area as shown

Select a capture area as shown

When you can see the Capture Controls, you know Ezvid is recording

CLICK TO STOP

You can play the game as normal while Ezvid is recording, but don't move the window, otherwise it will record the wrong part of the screen!

If the game seems jerky or unresponsive, this is because your computer is struggling to run the game and record it at the same time. To make it run more smoothly, try lowering some of Minecraft's details, effects and rendering distance in the "Options" screen.

When you're finished, click "Stop" on the video controls. Ezvid will process the video and then place it on the timeline.

If you've recorded multiple videos, you can move them around the timeline for editing. You can also use the "Record Voice" tool to add narration, use the "Add Text" tool to insert title cards and other notes, and the "Add Pictures or Video" tool to insert existing images or videos into your project.

You can preview your project by clicking the "Play" button on the left. You can add a name and description in the boxes in the top left.

This video project will remain open until you start a new one. When you finish your project, you can upload it to YouTube by clicking "Upload to YouTube" in the bottom right and following the login steps. If you're under 13, you'll need an adult to create a YouTube account for you!

Finally, if you want to get to the videos you've captured, you can find them in My Documents -> EZVid -> Projects -> [1 / 2 / etc...] / media. The videos are in WMV format.

When you're finished, click "Stop" and let Ezvid import your video

You can then preview and edit your video using the timeline

Remember to fill in details like the video title and description

PLANNING YOUR VIDEO

Now that you know how to record a video, you should think about what you actually want to record and why. Try to answer the following questions:

- How long should my video be?
- What am I trying to show people with my video?
- What can people learn from my video?
- What would I want to see if this was someone else's video?

Answering these questions should make it easier for you to decide what you want to put in your video.

Once you've made a few videos, you might want to start editing them more. You'll need a video-editing program to do this, but again don't download it without the permission of the PC owner!

There's a lot of competition for your video

VIDEO RECORDING TIPS

Some tasks in Minecraft take a long time but aren't very interesting. Rather than forcing viewers to sit through the whole thing, show yourself starting, pause the recording, then unpause it near the end so that you don't waste time on something uninteresting.

Don't use too many mods while making videos because this will confuse viewers about which version of the game you're using. If you do have mods or texture packs installed, explain so at the start!

Never use copyrighted music on your videos if you're uploading them to YouTube. The site will be able to tell and automatically delete your video! Most people stop watching a video after the first 10 seconds if they're not entertained. Make your intros as interesting or funny as possible!

You can edit your videos more using Windows Movie Maker

Make a really good video, and the views will clock up fast!

BLOCKDOKU

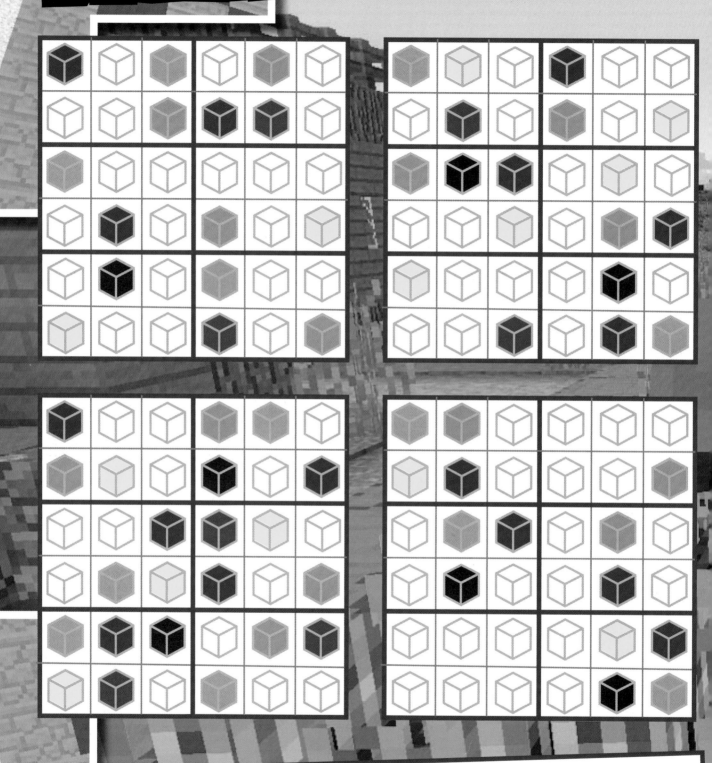

Can you colour in these grids of blocks following these three rules?

- Each square must contain a coloured block
- Each of the red rectangles must contain all six kinds of block
- No type of block can appear on any line twice, horizontally or vertically...

56

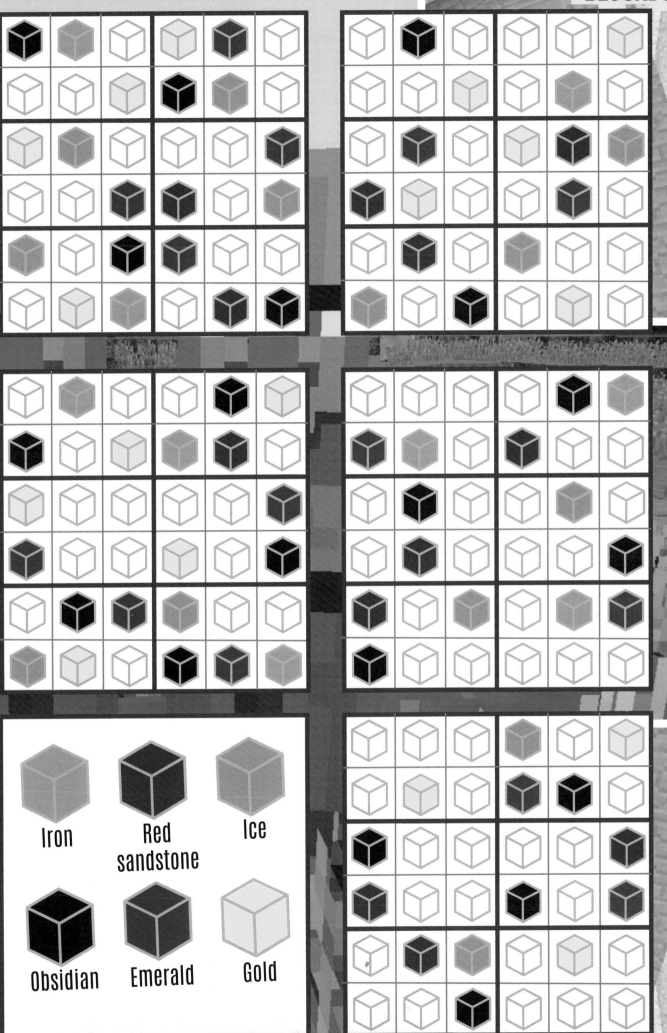

HOW TO COMPLETE MINECRAFT

Minecraft is an open-world game, where you can do anything you want, but did you know that there's also an "ending" to it?!

The end of Minecraft occurs when you defeat the ender dragon and return to the Overworld. As soon as you step inside, you get to read the mysterious End poem – a strange story apparently written by the endermen.

But how do you get to that point? To beat Minecraft, you have to follow these steps:

First, build a shelter and craft yourself some decent armour and tools. Each night, go out and kill endermen. You need to collect as many ender pearls as you can, but 64 should be more than enough.

Collect enough diamonds to craft a diamond pickaxe. You can mine for diamond ore, search treasure chests or make trades. You only need three, but the more you collect the better the armour and weapons you can craft.

Use the diamond pickaxe to mine obsidian and make a Nether portal.

You need at least 10 blocks, but aim for more than that so that you can create an exit inside the Nether.

Ignite your portal (a flint and steel is best for this) and enter the Nether. You don't HAVE to enchant your weapons and armour, but get used to it.

Find a Nether fortress in the Nether. You need to kill blazes and collect the blaze rods they drop.

Return to the Overworld, and craft your blaze rods into blaze powder.

Get a Nether portal built

Head to the Nether and find blazes

Start by killing endermen

Create eyes of ender and follow them to a stronghold

Find the End portal in a stronghold

Then you just have a dragon to kill!

■ Combine the blaze powder with ender pearls to create as many eyes of ender as you can. The minimum you need is 11, but that assumes nothing goes wrong – don't continue until you have double that amount!

■ Throw your eyes of ender and follow them to the nearest stronghold. Make sure you have at least 11 intact when you enter the stronghold!

■ Explore the stronghold until you find the End portal room. If you can't find one, look for a different stronghold and try again!

■ Fill the portal frame with eyes of ender. A portal needs 12 eyes in total to activate (but there should be at least one in there already).

■ You can now enter the End, but first load up on the strongest armour and weapons possible. If you can, bring some friends!

■ When you're ready, enter the portal to the End. Only do so when you're DEFINITELY prepared as, once you go in, the only way to get back is to defeat the ender dragon – or die trying!

■ Kill the ender dragon. If you manage this, you get 5,000 XP points! The exit portal will activate to take you back to the Overworld, and once you jump in you'll get to read the End poem and see Minecraft's "ending".

GET CRAFTY!

It's time to get creative again!
Have fun colouring in this awesome picture
of one of our favourite heroes – Steve!

60

SHHHH...!
EPIC TOP SECRET TIPS SECTION STARTS HERE!

Deserts have almost no plant life

DEEP OCEAN

Ocean biomes are twice as deep as normal oceans, and the only place you'll find ocean monuments.

DESERT

Deserts are made of sand above a base of sandstone. They have almost no animal or plant life, but also contain lots of structures – villages, wells, and desert temples.

EXTREME HILLS

Beneath the steep mountains of the extreme hills biomes, you'll find a lot more caves than usual. Plus, they're the only place where emerald ore can be found, not to mention the only place you'll encounter silverfish outside of strongholds.

BIOME SECRETS

You might think you know about all the biomes you can find in Minecraft – but do you know these secrets?

GRASS PLAINS

Grass plains are relatively flat and full of long grass, which often hides ravines, so take care! They spawn large numbers of peaceful mobs, and are a common place to find NPC villages. They're also one of two biomes that spawn horses.

Flower forests are full of plants

FLOWER FOREST

Flower forests are variants of normal forest biomes where the trees are replaced by flowers, including a number of rare plants you can't find anywhere else in the game.

ICE PLAINS

Ice plains are large, empty plains covered in snow with very few trees, and they're the only place in the game where you can find igloos!

ICE SPIKES

This rare variant of ice plains is full of large towers made of packed ice – a block that doesn't occur anywhere else in the game.

Jungles are densely packed

MESA

Mesas are rocky, colourful deserts, and the only place you can find red sand, red sandstone and stained clay.

JUNGLE

Jungle biomes consist of tall, thick trees with dense leaf cover. Melons, cocoa pods and ocelots only spawn in jungles. Trees are normally covered in vines, which you can climb. You'll also find jungle temples here.

MEGA TAIGA

A temperate forest of super-tall trees, the mega taiga biomes contain unique mossy boulders and podzol – a rare dirt type that can keep mushrooms alive in direct sunlight.

MUSHROOM ISLAND

One of the rarest biomes, mushroom islands are only found in the ocean and are made of mycelium instead of dirt. They're covered in all types of mushrooms, they're the only place where you can find mooshrooms, and no hostile mobs spawn there – not even underground!

SAVANNA

These warm grasslands are the only place you can find Acacia trees, and the second of two biomes in which horses spawn naturally.

ROOFED FOREST

Composed entirely of densely packed oak trees, roofed forests are the only place huge mushrooms spawn other than a mushroom island.

SAVANNA PLATEAU

A savanna variant with extreme, super-high mountains that often reach right above the clouds.

SWAMPLAND

Swamps have shallow, greenish water filled with lily pads, vines hanging off any trees, and lots of mushrooms. They're a good place to find clay, and the only place where witch huts are generated.

SUNFLOWER PLAINS

These variants of grass plains are patches of ground where lots of sunflowers grow. Remember, sunflowers always face the sun!

Baby zombies are faster than regular zombies and don't burn in sunlight.
Blazes are the only mob to take damage from snowballs.
Cave spiders are the only mob that can poison you.
Creepers turn into charged creepers when struck by lightning, which causes a much bigger explosion.
Elder guardians inflict the Mining Fatigue status, which makes it almost impossible to break blocks around you while they're still alive!
Endermen are the only mob that can carry blocks, and the only one to spawn in all three dimensions: the Overworld, the Nether and the End.

Baby zombies don't burn in sunlight

The smaller cave spider can poison you

MOB SECRETS

Every mob in Minecraft has its own secret or special attribute that you might not know about. Here's a list of interesting things about every regular enemy in the game!

A ghast in the Nether

The three sizes of magma cube

Endermites can appear when you teleport using an ender pearl – roughly one in 20 uses.
Evokers drop the totem of undying, which resurrects the holder after death!
Ghasts have the longest range of all mobs – they can hit you from 100 blocks away!
Guardian laser beams can't be dodged – the only way to block them is to put a block between you and the guardian before it fires!
Husks act like zombies but don't burn in sunlight. They also inflict the Hunger effect when they attack.
Illusioners will not cast the Blindness spell on the same opponent twice in a row.
Magma cubes are slightly more common in Nether fortresses than anywhere else in the Nether.

Phantoms only attack players who've not slept for three days or more, and are the only mob to appear in the End and the Overworld but not in the Nether.

Shulkers teleport if they come into contact with water.

Silverfish hide in blocks called monster eggs, which look like stone bricks or stone but break instantly.

Skeletons can collect weapons and armour if you drop it. If they wear a helmet, they won't burn up in sunlight.

Slimes won't spawn close to a player so you have to hike to find them, even if you're in the right place.

Spiders have the unique ability to climb walls, though they can be kept from doing so by using ice blocks.

Spider jockeys can be forced to separate if you knock them into water.

Strays spawn instead of skeletons in icy biomes, and shoot Slowness-tipped arrows instead of regular arrows.

Vindicators won't follow the player through iron doors.

Witches are 85% resistant to magic (meaning damage from enchantments and potions).

Wither skeletons are the only mob that has a chance of dropping its head when killed by the player.

Zombies will cluster around doors, and even break down wooden ones in normal and hard modes.

Zombie villagers can be cured using a splash Potion of Weakness and a golden apple.

Zombie pigmen will swap their golden swords for any better weapons they collect off the ground.

Shulkers hide inside purpur blocks

Silverfish hide in blocks

A regular skeleton and a stray

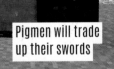

Pigmen will trade up their swords

Ender Dragon

A boss health bar

Put end crystals on the portal frame to resurrect the dragon

ALL BOSSES

Bosses are immune to most status effects, so don't waste precious potions or tipped arrows on them – you have to fight them the old-fashioned way!

They also don't have any trouble seeing through your magic, so hang onto your Invisibility potions!

You know you're in a boss fight when a health bar appears at the top of your screen. Once this starts, you have no choice but to fight or run away. Until killed, the boss will stick around forever!

BOSS SECRETS

Want to know a little more about the hardest mobs Minecraft has to offer? Wish you had some tips on how to defeat them? Well, good news – you can find their secrets right here!

Collect dragon's breath to make lingering potions

How to collect a dragon egg

THE ENDER DRAGON

If you destroy the end crystals while the dragon is charging from them, it will take a large amount of damage.

The dragon egg can be hatched by placing four end crystals on the portal.

You won't get 12,000 experience points for killing a dragon the second time – just 500!

You can collect the dragon's breath using glass bottles, then add it to splash potions to brew lingering potions.

Trying to break the dragon egg causes it to teleport, but if it teleports onto end stone, place a torch two blocks beneath it, then break the end stone beneath it. The egg will fall onto the torch and drop as an item.

THE WITHER

A random painting shows you how to place soul sand and skeleton skulls in order to summon a wither.

You can also find a secret image of the wither on chiseled red sandstone blocks, which can be crafted by combining two red sandstone slabs.

The wither is a lot weaker on the Java Edition than the Bedrock or Console Editions – 300 hit points instead of 600!

Once you summon a wither, you have 10 seconds to get out of the way!

When summoning a wither, the skeleton skulls must be the last part placed. You also can't summon a wither in Peaceful mode.

This painting is a clue to summoning the wither

Carved red sandstone also shows the wither

ELDER GUARDIANS

Elder guardians only despawn in Peaceful, so once you find a monument you'll have at least one elder guardian to fight, and no way to avoid it other than staying outside the monument!

The good news is that elder guardians won't respawn once killed.

One in 40 elder guardians will drop an extra fish as well as their normal raw fish drop.

Elder guardians will fight both players and squid, so they may be easier to fight in open ocean.

Elder guardians don't try to retreat if advanced upon by the player.

In advancements or achievements, you'll earn The Deep End for defeating your first elder guardian.

The wither arrives with a large bang

Elder guardians (left) are much bigger than normal guardians

Fossils are huge once uncovered

FOSSILS

Hidden under desert and swampland biomes, you can find fossils – the remains of strange dinosaur-like mobs that once roamed the Overworld. Constructed from bone blocks, they're more fun to excavate than they are useful, but half the thrill is finding one at all. Search 15-20 blocks beneath the surface and you'll hit one eventually.

DESERT TEMPLES

Desert temples are hard to miss, but did you know inside each one there's a pit with four chests beneath the blue clay block? At the bottom of the pit is a pressure plate that will activate nine blocks of TNT, so remember to destroy that before you accidentally set it off!

Desert temples have rare stained clay and chiselled sandstone

HIDDEN FINDS

Only the most seasoned adventurers will have ticked EVERYTHING off this list. The rest of you, get ready to learn the secrets of Minecraft's best hidden finds.

Don't miss your chance to get emerald ore!

MOB HEADS

Did you know zombies, skeletons, and creepers can drop their heads when they die,? If you trick a charged creeper into blowing up and killing these mobs close by, they may drop their heads. Mob heads can be placed as blocks or worn as masks to reduce your detection by that mob!

EMERALDS

Emeralds only appear in their ore form in the deepest caves beneath the extreme hills biome. Once you're deep enough, they're more common than diamonds, but as they appear in single-block veins, they can be tough to find!

Wear mob heads to scare your friends!

Play music discs in a jukebox

CHAINMAIL ARMOUR

It's impossible to craft this rare armour, but occasionally a mob (which will drop it only in very rare circumstances) can be found wearing it. The only realistic way to get hold of it is to trade with a blacksmith villager. Chainmail armour is only slightly weaker than iron armour but easier to enchant than gold armour.

MUSIC DISCS

There are 12 music discs in Minecraft, which you can play in a jukebox to hear a specific tune. Two of them can be found in chests as treasure, but the other nine only drop if you trick a skeleton into killing a creeper with its arrow!

Chainmail armour looks odd

Alliums in a flower forest

SPONGES

These blocks absorb water (if dry!) and are only found in ocean monuments. Some monuments have rooms filled with sponges which you can collect by mining them. Elder guardians also drop a sponge when killed. To use a wet sponge, you have to dry it out in a furnace, place it next to some water, and the sponge will suck it up.

ALLIUM FLOWERS

The flower forest is a rare variant biome where trees are almost entirely replaced with different types of flower. However, one type of flower ONLY appears in flower forests, and that's the pink allium. You can easily spot them, and it's worth collecting them when you do because you won't get many chances.

You can find sponges in a monument

DESIGN YOUR NEXT BUILD HERE

You made it through our top secret section? Awesome! Hopefully, by now you're inspired to design a new build for yourself too! Here's a page just so you can map something out - happy designing!

Aaargh! This Ice Plains biome is crawling with hostile mobs!

CRAFTY CALLUM

IN THE SNOW GOLEM!

Callum is in the middle of a snow ball fight with some friendly neighbourhood mobs!

Urgh! I feel like a Snow Golem!

Ha ha! No time to Chillax Callum! Ready for more?

SNOW GOLEM! That's it!

I need to defend my base! This Snow Golem will help me hold the fort!

Callum makes a run for it, but...

BUS STOP

CLANG!

Yeouch! Who put that there?

SNAP!

SNAP!

Oh no! Here come the Strays! I'd better scarper.

Aargh! I can't move. It looks like one of the Strays has hit me with an arrow of slowness! I'm done for!

STOP

Wargle!

BRRRRRR! Oh no the game has frozen!

Ha ha! We gotcha Callum!

Yeah! SNOW JOKE! LOL!

SHIVER!

SHIVER!

And so...

Phew! I've managed to respawn readers!

And I've chosen a boiling hot desert biome to play in this time! Chuckle!

END!

DID YOU HEAR ABOUT THE CREEPER THROWING A BIRTHDAY PARTY FOR ALEX?
IT WAS A SSSSSSSSSSSSSSURPRISE!

WHY DID STEVE FAIL HIS EXAMS?
HE'D BLOCKED EVERYTHING OUT!

IN WHAT COUNTRY ARE YOU MOST LIKELY TO FIND GHASTS?
THE NETHER-LANDS!

WHAT SPORT DO WOLVES LIKE?
TEN PIN HOWLING!

MINECRAFT JOKES!

DID YOU HEAR ABOUT THE MINECRAFT TRAIN?
IT STOPPED WHEN IT GOT TO THE ENDER THE LINE!

WHAT DID STEVE SAY TO ALEX WHEN HE GAVE HER SOME FOOD?
HAVE A HEART!

WHAT DID THE MOB SAY WHEN HE ASKED STEVE AND ALEX TO THE CINEMA?
I'M GOING WITHER WITHOUT YOU!

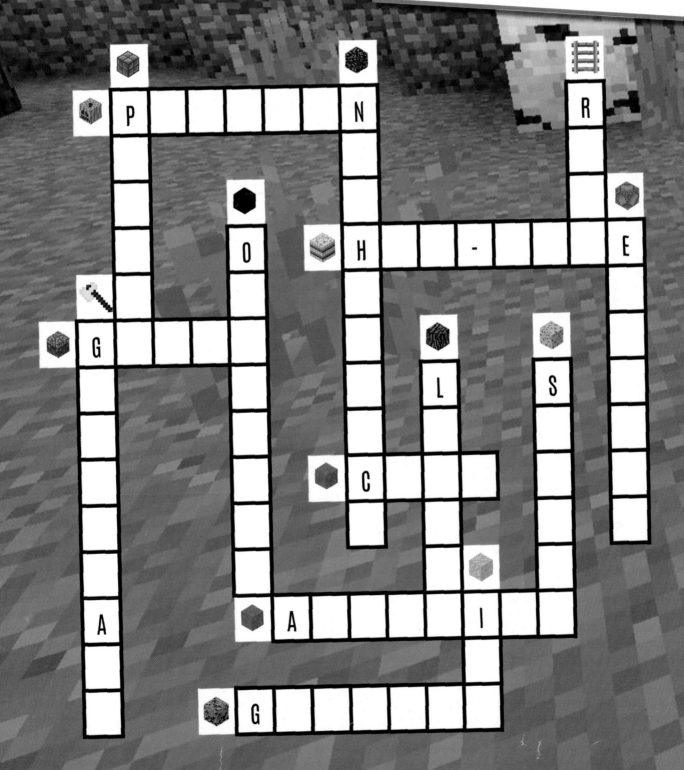

PICTURE BLOCKWORD!

Can you fill out this word grid by identifying the blocks at the beginning of each line? We've put in the first letters to help you out, but just how much of a Minecraft expert are you?!

ADD-ONS

Available for the Bedrock Edition, Add-Ons are small mods that don't require any extra software to work. You can download sample Add-Ons from minecraft.net/en/addons, where you'll find two official ones – Alien Invasion and Castle Siege – plus the unmodified behaviour files and resource packs. Downloading these will help you learn how to install Add-Ons, but it also gives you the tools to start making your own!

Add-Ons come as ".mcworld" or ".mcpack" files, which can contain three main elements: the map you play in, any modified behaviour files, and any modified resource packs. This means that some are small, and some are large. The exact way to install them differs, based on the version you play, so we've got a guide coming right up!

Add-Ons have existed for a while so there are lots of user-created ones to download from mcpedl.com and minecraftpe-mods.com. As long as you have the right version of Minecraft (Bedrock Edition) installed – and not the Legacy Console or Java Editions – you just have to click the correct links to get started.

ADD-ONS, MO

One of the coolest things about Minecraft is that you don't have to wait for the people in charge to add things to it. Tonnes of programmers and artists build their own Add-Ons, mods and extras for the game! But what are they making, and where can you find it?

An Add-On makes this villager ride a cow

The official Add-Ons

ALIEN INVASION

You may recognise this one from our E3 demo: it's an action-packed scenario where you'll need to defend a city from alien invasion! Watch our devs play it here!

CASTLE SIEGE

This Add-On was made by the awesome Sethbling with Blockworks and Mindcrack. Defend the fort from the mob horde or join the monsters and crash the keep! Watch a clip here!

Find and manage installed Add-Ons in the menus

Settings
Touch
General
Profile
Video
Audio
Global Resources
Storage
Language

Storage

World Templates
16.2MB – 1 Item

Resource Packs
3.8MB – 1 Item

Jurassic Craft v3.1 ...
Version 0.0.1
Add-On by Gona   3.8MB

Behavior Packs
0.31MB – 1 Item

Jurassic Craft v3.1 ...
Version 0.0.1
Add-On by Gona   0.31MB

Resource Pack
fully Imported

How to know an
installation worked

Select an Add-On
here to use it

A dragon in the
Overworld - possible
with Add-Ons!

DS & EXTRAS

HOW TO INSTALL ADD-ONS

Installing Add-Ons is simple, but it's different for every version. Here's how to do it on the most popular versions:

WINDOWS 10

1. Run Minecraft: Windows 10 Edition.
2. Find the .mcworld file you want to use and double-click it.
3. The Add-On should open in Minecraft and install automatically.

IPHONE, IPAD & IPOD TOUCH

1. Run Minecraft: Pocket Edition.
2. Switch out of the app and open the .mcworld file (from your email, iCloud account, etc).
3. Choose to open the file in Minecraft: Pocket Edition by selecting the Minecraft icon from the list of apps.
4. The Add-On should open in Minecraft and install automatically.

ANDROID

1. Run Minecraft: Pocket Edition.
2. Switch out of the app and download the .mcworld file on your device.
3. Open the Settings app and select Storage > Explore. Select the directory where the file was downloaded to (usually "Download") then open it.
4. The Add-On should open in Minecraft and install automatically.

In all versions, if you open an Add-On that contains a world, the game will load that world automatically. If you're opening a .mcpack file that contains just resources, the game will alert you that it's been added, but you won't see it until you activate it in the settings.

To exit an Add-On world, close it and quit to the main menu. To remove an Add-On resource pack, look in Settings.

MODS

If you're running the Java Edition, there's a different way to make modifications to your game. This involves running a program called Forge, so first you need to check with the computer's owner that you're allowed to install the software.

Next, you need to make sure you have the full version of Minecraft for PC (or Mac, or Linux) installed. The Bedrock Edition doesn't support Forge mods.

Now download the version of Forge that matches your version of Minecraft from files.minecraftforge.net. To check which version of Minecraft you're running, open the launcher and look at the base of the "play" button. Forge and individual mods will need to be compatible with this version number, so make a note of it!

If you're using the latest version of Minecraft, download the "recommended" version of Forge. The easiest way to install it is to use the installer, so click on that, download the file, and run it.

When it runs, you'll see the launch screen. Select "Install client" and click "OK". It will download the necessary files and install a Forge profile in your Minecraft launcher.

To open Minecraft with Forge installed, you have to change the profile (click the arrow on the right of your "Play" button) to the Forge profile, as pictured. When you click "Play", it will download the necessary files and launch Minecraft.

If Forge has been installed correctly, the loading screen will be a little different. The Minecraft title screen should also show information on the number of mods installed, and show a "Mods" button.

Mods can easily add new blocks or mobs

Downloads for Minecraft Forge - MC 1.12.2

Download Latest
1.12.2 - 14.23.2.2624

Download Recommended
1.12.2 - 14.23.2.2611

Windows Installer
Changelog
Installer
Mdk
Universal

Windows Installer
Changelog
Install
Mdk
Univer

All Note

Click the recommended installer!

The list below are for getting a *specific* version of Forge. Unless you need this, prefer the links to latest and recommen

+ Show all Versions

Select the Forge profile

Latest snapshot
17w06a

forge
1.10.2-forge1.10.2-12.18.1.2011

1.7.4
1.7.4

Explore the con

PLAY
1.11.2 - Latest release

The title screen should look like this

Normal | A-Z | Z-A

Mod List

Minecraft Coder Pack
9.19
0 child mods

Forge Mod Loader
8.0.99.99
0 child mods

Minecraft Forge
12.18.1.2011
0 child mods

Installed mods show up in here

A dragon in the Overworld - possible with Add-Ons!

Before you open any existing worlds, make a backup copy – some mods add extra blocks and items, so if you open an existing world with a mod activated, it might become broken when you return without the mod activated.

Now you're ready to install some mods! They can be found on lots of websites, but check the version number first, otherwise they might be broken!

When you download a mod, you should get a ".jar" file, though it might be stored in a ZIP file! You need to copy that file into your Minecraft mods directory, which is located somewhere like C:\Users\[your username]\AppData\Roaming\.minecraft\mods

Once you've done that, launch Minecraft with your Forge profile as before. On the title screen, click the "Mods" button and you should see a list of your installed mods. Forge has a few mods installed by default, which you must leave enabled. If any mods are missing, it's probably because they aren't compatible with the current version of Minecraft and/or Forge.

Click on the mods to enable/disable them, and click "Done" when you're finished. You can now start a single or multiplayer game as normal.

If you want to completely remove a mod, browse to the "mods" directory given above and simply delete its .jar file.

To return to unmodded Minecraft, just change your profile to the "latest release" one in the Minecraft launcher.

As for where to get mods, visit www.minecraftmods.com or minecraftsix.com – both should have plenty!

10 QUICK BUILD TIPS

Building stuff in Minecraft is always great fun. But how can you make sure your projects go smoothly, look cool and don't waste previous materials? Simply follow this advice!

10 Build multiple furnaces
It takes a few seconds to smelt a single block, so build four or five furnaces, and you'll soon have more resources than you need!

9 Lay slabs for flooring
Slabs double the amount of space you can cover with your blocks – three stone blocks make six stone slabs.

8 Enchant your tools
Making your hardware faster and more durable can massively reduce the amount of time your projects take!

7 Vary your materials
Don't use a single block type – use variants to add a pattern and make walls and floors more interesting.

6 Highlight doors and windows
You'll be surprised how much better they look if you mark them out with some other type of block beneath or above.

5 Light rooms properly
Leave no dark corners – mobs can spawn in even the smallest spaces!

4 Make a plan first
Before you start building your house, take a moment to map it out on the ground to get an idea of its eventual size and shape!

3 Remember the L rule
If you're building a house or base, don't make it square or rectangular – make it L-shaped and it will look better inside AND outside.

2 Hide your lighting
Build glowstone or lanterns into the floor, and cover them with carpet. Your rooms will be bright and there'll be no unsightly torches around.

1 Keep trying!
If a building doesn't turn out how you want, don't give up. It's easier to improve something that's already built than to make the perfect build straight away!

```
F U R N A C E S
L L C R M R H L
O C E L O T O V
W Z S C R S G S
E J E R E B W E
R C C A V X A C
F H R F S I R R
O A E T N P T E
S W I Q R I T Y O I S T E V E B
Z L G B E N S C W X D D A X E O
C L I R S M A A G E P O X U W L
T C X M T A O L O L X B M V I
K H F I E I D L L A E R T K R O
J E G H A L M U E R X P M I P N
H A U C R A J M M T P I E Y O U
B T Y V T R Y G D J L G B B Y N
H S E N H M D L B I O M E R W R
Y F R E R O M W H V R E I L O V
I G L O O U E P V Z A N J G M I
      P R N P D T T K
      O B D M F W I G
      D H E A O N O O
      H C R G S S N L
      R R D M S F Z D
      F E R A I E Z T
      X E A C L P O H
      G P G U P V O R
      T E O B W S S O
      S R N E S H Z N
      U K E D B Q I E
```

WORDSEARCH

Can you find these words?

ARTHROPOD
AXE
BIOME
CHAINMAIL
ARMOUR
CHEATS
CRAFTY
CALLUM
CREEPER
ENDER
DRAGON
EXPLORATION
FLOWER
FOREST
FOSSIL
FURNACES
GOLD THRONE
HOGWARTS
IGLOO
MAGMA CUBE
OCELOT
PIGMEN
PIXEL ART
POTION
SECRET DOOR
SECRETS
SLIME
SNOW GOLEM
STEVE

1 AN EASY ONE TO START WITH. WHICH OF THESE MAIN CHARACTERS CAN'T YOU PLAY AS IN MINECRAFT?

A) Steve
B) Alex
C) Brian

2 WHAT DO YOU NEED FOR A 3X3 CRAFTING GRID IN THE GAME?

A) A crafting garage
B) A crafting cavern
C) A crafting table

3 WHICH OF THESE MOBS IS HOSTILE IN MINECRAFT?

A) Wolf
B) Ghast
C) Rabbit

THE BIG MINECRAFT QUIZ

Reckon you know your way around Minecraft? See if you can answer our questions – and don't forget to check how you measure up at the end!

4 WHAT IS THE NAME OF THE MINECRAFT ADVENTURE GAME SERIES OF GAMES?

A) Minecraft: Adventure Mode
B) Minecraft: Quest Mode
C) Minecraft: Story Mode

5 WHAT KIND OF STONE DO YOU NEED FOR ELECTRICAL POWER IN MINECRAFT?

A) Bluestone
B) Greenstone
C) Redstone

9 WHICH OF THESE IS A GHOSTLY FIGURE RUMOURED TO HAVE BEEN SEEN IN MINECRAFT?

A) Slimer
B) Blinky
C) Herobrine

10 WHICH ANIMAL ARE MOOSHROOMS ARE VARIANT OF?

A) Pigs
B) Cows
C) Dolphins

8 WHO DO YOU TRADE WITH IN THE GAME?

A) Villagers
B) Creepers
C) Golems

7 WHICH OF THESE IS NOT A GAME MODE IN MINECRAFT?

A) Simulation
B) Creative
C) Survival

11 WHICH OF THESE WILL YOU NATURALLY FIND IN THE END?

A) Shulkers
B) Villagers
C) Ocelots

12 WHAT DOES A PIG TURN INTO IF STRUCK BY LIGHTNING?

A) Zombie pigman
B) Hostile pumpkin
C) Mooshroom

6 WHAT IS THE ANNUAL OFFICIAL MINECRAFT CONVENTION KNOWN AS?

A) Minecon
B) Mineshow
C) Minecraft Show

13 WHICH OF THESE IS A MINECRAFT MULTIPLAYER SERVER?

A) Minecraft Realms
B) Minecraft Networks
C) Minecraft Switch It Off And On

14 WHAT TWO TYPES OF GOLEM CAN YOU FIND IN MINECRAFT?

A) Iron and fire
B) Snow and iron
C) Snow and fire

15 WHAT IS THE SPECIAL VERSION OF MINECRAFT USED IN MANY SCHOOL CLASSROOMS CALLED?

A) Minecraft: Better Than Lessons Edition
B) Minecraft: Schools Special
C) Minecraft: Education Edition

16 WHICH OF THESE BIOMES IS THE HOTTEST?

A) Extreme hills
B) Frozen ocean
C) Swampland

17 WHICH OF THESE IS THE NAME OF A MINECRAFT UPDATE?

A) Update Aquatic
B) Update Armada
C) Update Antique

18 WHERE WILL YOU FIND A GUARDIAN?

A)   In the sky
B)   On land
C)   Underwater

19 WHICH COMPANY BOUGHT UP MOJANG, THE MAKERS OF MINECRAFT, FOR $2.5BN?!

A)   Odeon
B)   Microsoft
C)   Apple

20 FINALLY, MINECRAFT IS:

A)   Rubbish
B)   Not bad
C)   Brilliant!

ANSWERS!

HOW DID YOU DO?!
20   Brilliant! You're an epic Minecraft expert!
15-19 You know your stuff, don't you? Top work!
10-14 You're well on the way to becoming a Minecraft genius – well done!
4-9   You're getting there, but still a few things to learn! The only option? More Minecraft!
0-3   Eeek! All we can suggest is that you play lots and lots and lots of Minecraft! Can't be bad, right?!

1	C
2	C
3	B
4	C
5	C
6	A
7	A
8	A
9	C
10	B
11	A
12	B
13	C
14	A
15	A
16	C
17	A
18	C
19	B
20	C

CRAFTY PICTURE GRID

Use the grid from the first picture to help you copy Jesse into the empty squares, then colour her in however you like!

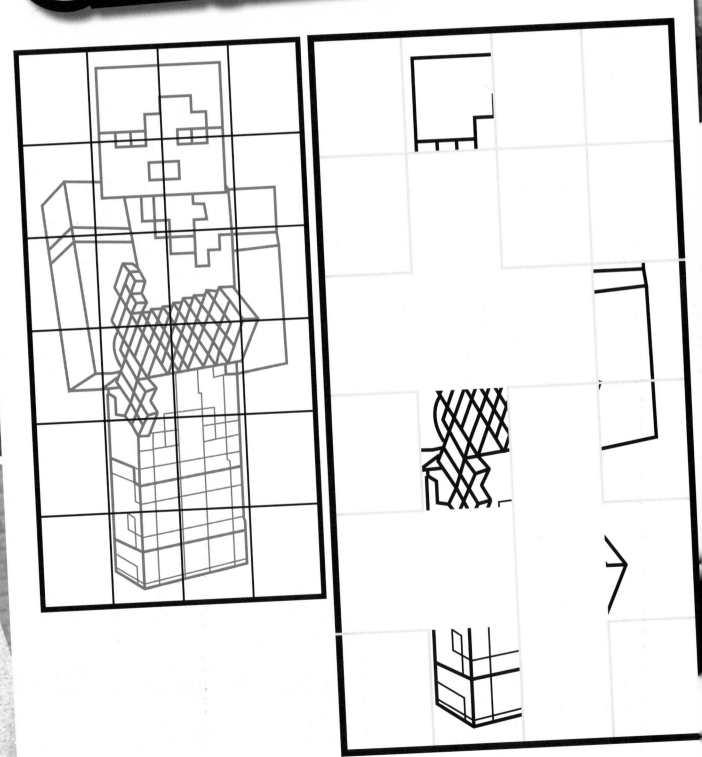

SPOT-THE-DIFFERENCE

We've made eight sneaky changes to the second picture – can you spot them?

87

EXPERT

Want to play Minecraft like a pro? We've got FOUR pages of tips that will help you survive longer, beat more mobs, collect more loot, and show your friends that you are, without doubt, the #1 Minecraft expert around!

You get up to 28 experience for killing slimes

Witches will drink potions when injured

No good can come of killing villagers

MOB TIPS

■ If you don't kill a silverfish in one hit, others nearby will emerge to help it defend itself by attacking you. A diamond sword should be strong enough to kill them at a single stroke!

■ Because of the way slimes and magma cubes divide into smaller versions, you can collect up to 28 experience from each large one you encounter.

■ Don't build a portal near your home or base unless you're looking for a fight, as they can cause pigmen to spawn. Instead, build one in a large chamber or pit to keep mobs from getting out!

■ You can use potions to restore your health in a fight, but so can witches! Don't pause to heal yourself in a fight with one, because you'll only lose whatever progress you've made.

■ Killing friendly villagers has no positive effect. They don't drop anything and it will lower your reputation with other villagers, so they might refuse to trade with you.

■ Be careful when wandering around forests as the shade of trees hides zombies from the sun, allowing them to remain alive during the day. Make them chase you into the light so that they set on fire!

■ Endermen HATE water – rain injures them and they won't teleport into water, so use that knowledge to keep them away from you.

TIPS

You can spend lots of XP on an anvil

MAGIC TIPS

◼ If you give a fishing rod the Mending enchantment, it can be used forever because catching anything with the rod will repair it at least as much as it's being damaged.

◼ One piece of blaze powder can power around 20 brewing operations, so you don't need huge amounts of it when you're making potions. However, blaze powder is rare and useful, so we'd recommend collecting as much as you can.

◼ You can use a cauldron to fill water bottles in the Nether, where there's no other source of water for brewing.

◼ You don't have to craft glass bottles – you can collect them by killing witches, who drop 0-6 empty bottles when they die. In fact, witches drop most of the stuff you need for brewing awesome potions!

◼ It's possible to remove the pumpkin from a snow golem's head using a pair of shears.

◼ If a village has over 10 inhabitants and at least 21 doors, an iron golem can spawn automatically to protect it from attacking mobs (or players!) so take care when you're fighting mobs – hit a villager and you might have to contend with their defender.

◼ The most powerful enchantments require you to spend 30 levels, while the most powerful uses of the anvil allow you to spend up to 39. If you have any more than that, it's worth spending them as soon as possible – each experience level takes longer to reach than the last, so the higher a level, the more it "costs" you per operation.

Fish forever with the Mending enchantment

A snow golem with no mask

Make your
own paths

Cobwebs can
hide spawners

EXPLORATION TIPS

■ If you want to make paths or roads to show you a common route, you can use the alternate action on a shovel to create a path.

■ Gravel can often fall into caves, creating an apparent dead end, so it's always worth mining through gravel if it appears your way is blocked. Just don't stand under it when it drops!

■ You can use a bucket of water as a portable "elevator". Swimming up and down water flows is quicker than building a staircase!

■ In single-player mode, entering the Nether causes time to freeze in the Overworld, and vice versa. Crops won't grow, and any mobs or items you leave behind will stay where they were until you return.

■ Getting loot safely means paying attention to your surroundings.

In abandoned mines, there's always a monster spawner at the centre of a mass of cobwebs, for example, while in Nether fortresses they appear by corners where mobs could be lurking...

■ If you want to explore the ocean floor, place doors and fence posts underwater to create "airlocks" that let you breathe without returning to the surface.

■ Steak and porkchops are the most efficient way to regain health when exploring, not least because they stack in your inventory! Rabbit stew and cakes restore more health, but you can only carry one of each in an inventory slot.

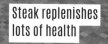

Steak replenishes
lots of health

Horses heal by eating hay

■ You can't eat most food when the hunger bar is full. The three foods you CAN eat are chorus fruit, golden apples and milk, because they all have beneficial effects other than restoring your hunger bar.

■ There are seven base colours and five types of marking for horses, making a total of 35 distinct variants.

■ One in every 50 potato plants you harvest will drop a poison potato, which is slightly greener than a normal potato and can't be planted or baked. If you eat a poisonous potato, you have a 60% chance (three in five) of getting the Poison effect for four seconds, which will drain three health points.

■ A bucket of lava is 12 times better than a piece of coal for powering a furnace, so use them for your smelting if you're low on coal and don't want to waste time mining.

■ You can sprint straight over one-block gaps without stopping.

STRANGE FACTS

■ Chickens are the only non-hostile mob that can spawn in the Nether. This is because baby zombie pigmen have a small chance of spawning as chicken jockeys. The only other mob you can find in both the Overworld and the Nether are skeletons, which appear in Nether fortresses.

■ Hay bales are the only blocks that can be eaten by mobs. They heal up to 10 hearts when fed to a horse, donkey or mule, making them the most efficient way to restore their health.

Horses have many markings and colours

Lava buckets burn for a long time

ANSWERS

How did you do against our pages of pesky puzzles? Let's find out!

SPOT-THE-DIFFERENCE
Page 15

MEGA MAZE
Page 33

BLOCKDOKU
Page 56

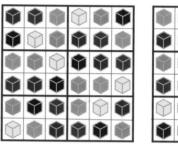

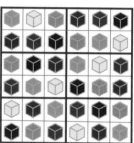

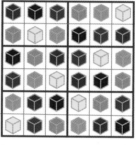

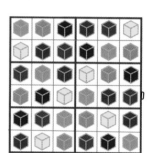

Page 57

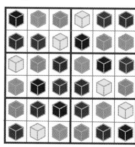

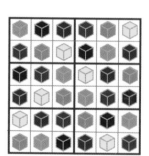

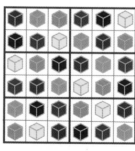

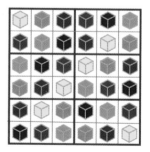

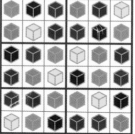

CRAFYGRAMS
Page 39

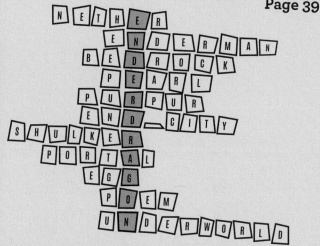

N E T H E R
E N D E R M A N
B E D R O C K
P E A R L
P U R P U R
E N D _ C I T Y
S H U L K E R
P O R T A L
E G G
P O E M
U N D E R W O R L D

WORDSEARCH
Page 81

BLOCKWORD
Page 75

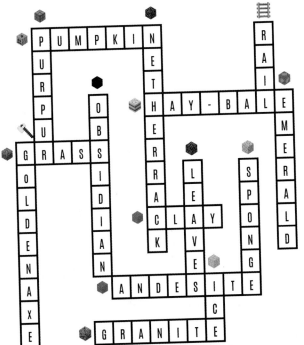

SPOT-THE-DIFFERENCE
Page 87